Visions of the Buffalo People

as told by
Linda Little Wolf

Pelican Publishing Company
Gretna 2003

First published by Syncopated Press, 2000
Published by arrangement with the author by
    Pelican Publishing Company, Inc., 2003

First edition, 2000
First Pelican edition, 2003

*The word "Pelican" and the depiction of a pelican are trademarks
of Pelican Publishing Company, Inc., and are registered in the
U.S. Patent and Trademark Office.*

Cover painting: Five Cent Piece *by David Behrens; used by permission*
Illustrations by Kimberly Graham

Printed in the United States of America

Published by Pelican Publishing Company, Inc.
1000 Burmaster Street, Gretna, Louisiana 70053

Table OF CONTENTS

In memory of Second Voice Coyote Woman (Leslie).

Nine years ago, just by chance, two young women met. Like little children, we invented, planned and dreamed about a great adventure. Your determination and your skillful hands brought our dreams to reality and my life was forever changed. I became your life-size Indian dress-up "doll," while you became my mentor and my best friend.

I watched as you graciously accepted life's challenges, touching the hearts of many with your strength, courage and dignity. Even during your illness, you remained completely focused on those who loved and needed you.

This is my promise – to keep your legacy alive, knowing that you are with me always. Side-by-side, we will continue our great adventure.

My deepest appreciation is extended to designer and illustrator, Kimberly Graham, artist David Behrens, photographer Wendy Wilson, consultant Vikki Ottrando, and Pelican Publishing Company. Their dedication, patience and tremendous talents transformed my historical lectures and ancient stories into a visual parade filled with the wisdom of my ancestors.

Thank you, for enabling my voice to touch the hearts and minds of youth worldwide.

LINDA LITTLE WOLF

Hiyakabidomi (HEE-YAH-KAH-BEE-DOE-MEE)

GREETINGS TO ALL LIVING THINGS IN THE UNIVERSE.

I am Linda Little Wolf. My ancestors, the Sioux, were one of many Native American peoples that called the Great Plains of North America their home.

Close your eyes. Picture a copper-skinned Indian brave galloping after a buffalo herd astride his loyal horse. He is dressed in fringed deerskin garments. His bow is drawn and ready to bring down a great humpbacked beast. This is our romantic ideal of the Plains Indian. But this was not always their way of life.

Early Plains Indians did not have horses. Horses became extinct on the North American continent approximately ten thousand years ago. For many centuries, the Plains Indians survived on foot as wandering nomads. It was a harsh and difficult life as they struggled to find food and shelter.

Spanish explorers first re-introduced horses to North America in the 1500s. A few hundred years later, the Plains Indians possessed horses in large numbers. This was the beginning of the Golden Era of the Horse.

The horse transformed the life and culture of the Plains Indians. Now on horseback, mounted hunters could follow the migrating buffalo herds farther and faster. Serving also as a pack animal, the horse allowed them to carry larger amounts of food and own more possessions. Because they no longer needed to spend all their time hunting, the hunters had more free time. They used this time to plan, make and celebrate warfare. The horse also represented wealth. Stealing horses from neighboring tribes became an honorable act.

Come with me now as we take a journey back through time and experience **Visions of the Buffalo People**.

Daily Life
WITHOUT A HORSE

The Great Plains covered nearly one million square miles. It reached from the foothills of the Rocky Mountains and stretched eastward to the woodlands of the Mississippi Valley. The northern edge of the Great Plains was in Alberta, Canada. The southern border of the Great Plains was found in central Texas.

For thousands of years, small nomadic tribes fought to survive on the Great Plains. The land was as dangerous as it was beautiful. It was a constant struggle in every season. Summer brought violent thunderstorms and tornadoes. Winters represented severe blizzards and huge snowfalls. The weather was unpredictable and full of peril for these simple people.

The buffalo was the key to human life on the Great Plains. The gigantic herds could darken the horizon for miles as they passed by. Successfully bringing down a buffalo meant the tiny band would survive for another week. It was dangerous hunting the great beasts on foot. Often, the hunters were unsuccessful and there was no meat for the cooking pot. The nomadic tribes suffered from many illnesses because they did not have enough protein in their diet. During this period the human population was never more than 10,000 – dispersed in small bands across the vast plains.

Tribes of the Great Plains

This map show approximate territories and language groups about the year 1800. After that, all tribes lost territory and some moved.

Tribes Key:

1 Sarcee
2 Plains Cree
3 Blackfeet
4 Gros Ventre
5 Assiniboin
6 Plains Ojibwa
7 Crow
8 Teton Sioux
9 Hidatsa
10 Mandan
11 Arikara
12 Yanktonai Sioux
13 Santee Sioux
14 Cheyenne
15 Ponca
16 Omaha
17 Yankton Sioux
18 Iowa
19 Oto
20 Pawnee
21 Arapaho
22 Kansa
23 Missouria
24 Kiowa
25 Kiowa-Apache
26 Osage
27 Comanche
28 Wichita
29 Quapaw
30 Lipan Aache
31 Tonkawa
32 Kitsai

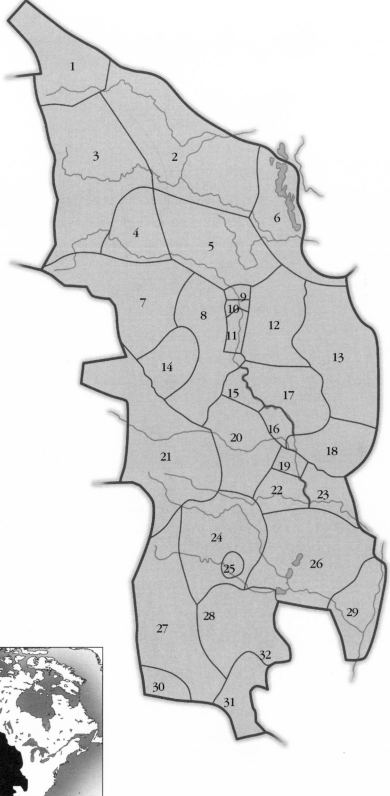

LIFE FOR THE NOMADS

The nomadic Plains people followed the migrating herds of buffalo. Dispersed in hundreds of small bands, they set up temporary camps in tents, called tipis. It was a difficult life. The entire tribe traveled on foot 15-20 miles every day of their lives to follow Tatanka. To make travel easier, they domesticated the dog to serve as a pack animal.

The dog wore a crude packsaddle over its shoulders. Attached to the saddle were two long poles that dragged along the ground as an A-shaped sled. French explorers that came to North America named this invention a *travois* (tra-voy). A sturdy dog could haul a travois filled with 75 pounds of dried buffalo meat and the few other possessions of the tribe.

The travois pulled by dogs determined the size of the tipi, since the travois poles also doubled as tipi poles. Tipis of this era were smaller than the ones we are accustomed to during the Golden Era of the Horse.

Hunting the buffalo on foot was difficult and dangerous for the early Plains Indians. Hunters used a combination of a stone-tipped thrusting spear and a spear-thrower called an *atlatal*. The atlatal was a shaft of wood or bone about two feet long. It allowed the hunter to throw the spear farther and with more power than using his arm alone.

Hunters also used cunning to get closer to the herd. Wearing a buffalo hide or wolf pelt, the hunters stalked the herd in disguise until they were close enough to throw their spears.

To help ensure there was enough meat to survive the winter, several bands would come together in late September. The hunters would work together for a month or so and then each band would go its own way. Sometimes they would stampede an entire herd over a cliff in a mass kill.

These hunting tools and methods endured for centuries. Many times the hunters returned unsuccessful. To make up for the lack of meat, tribes on the edge of the Great Plains would often settle in one place for a season. Here they would supplement their diet by hunting small game, fishing, picking nuts and berries, and harvesting other wild plants. Because of the limited food supply, the nomads were often close to starvation. This is the major reason that family groups remained small.

Although life on the Great Plains remained almost unchanged for centuries, the introduction of the horse would permanently change their culture and way of life forever.

BUILD YOUR OWN TIPI

ITEMS NEEDED:

Pencil

String or yarn

Clear tape

9 drinking straws or small wooden sticks (tipi poles)

1 large brown paper grocery bag

Crayons, markers, paint

INSTRUCTIONS:

1. The key to creating your own tipi is to draw a perfect circle. You can easily trace a circle by attaching a string to your pencil and hold the string in the center as you draw.

2. Cut out the circle from the paper bag. Crinkle the paper to give it the look of leather.

3. Lay the circle on a flat surface and cut out a triangle approximately $\frac{1}{8}$ of the circle. (Save this scrap, you can use it later to make a flap (door) for your tipi!)

4. Cut a small circle (1 inch in diameter) from the center of the circle for the poles.

5. Decorate the tipi cover with crayons, markers or paint.

6. Stand up the tipi poles and wrap the cover around them. Tape the cover together with clear tape.

A Project

Language
AS THEY SPOKE

The early Plains Indians did not have a written language. They only spoke their language and passed along the customs, traditions, and history of their people through oral communication. However, many tribes used drawings to document day-to-day life and important events, such as hunting expeditions and battles with the enemy. These primitive sketches were usually painted by a family member on tanned buffalo, elk, or deer hides and recorded the events that took place in a single year. Plains people called one year a "winter." The tanned hide displaying the pictographic history of a particular year was called a "winter count." It was only in the last century that many languages were transformed in to a written language.

Below is an illustration of a "winter count." This elk robe displays a pictographic history of one Indian brave's record of his hunts. The top shows the various horses used and some fellow tribal members who accompanied the owner on his hunts. The bottom dots record each individual hunt of that year.

The tribes of the Great Plains spoke many different and unique languages.

Practice counting in the language of the Arapaho, using the phonetic pronunciation guide.

NUMBERS

One	jaa-saa-ye
Two	neesh
Three	naa-sau
Four	ye-ain
Five	yaw-thawn
Six	ne-daw-dahx
Seven	ne-sau-dahx
Eight	naasau-dahx
Nine	thi-ah-dahx
Ten	baa-daa-dahx

Now learn to count in the Lakota Sioux language.

NUMBERS

		Pronounced:
One	wanji	wahn jee
Two	nupa	noo pah
Three	yamni	yah mnee
Four	topa	toh pah
Five	zaptan	zahp tahn
Six	`sakpe	shah kpay
Seven	`sakowin	shah koe ween
Eight	`saglohan	shah glow hahn
Nine	nepcunka	nape chun kah
Ten	wikcemna	week chay mnah

AND HOW DO YOU SAY...

Try your language skills with more Lakota Sioux.

COLORS

		Pronounced:
Blue	to	doe
Green	zito	zee doe
White	ska	skah
Pink	`samna	shah mnah
Red	`sa	shah
Black	sapa	sah pah
Yellow	zi	zee

ANIMALS

		Pronounced:
Dog	`sunka	shoon kah
Horse	`sunka tanka	shoon kah dahn kah
Wolf	`sungmanitu tanka	shoong mah nee doo dahn kah
Buffalo	tatanka	dah dahn kah
Coyote	`sungmahetu	shoong mah hay doo
Bear	mato	mah toe
Eagle	wambli	wahm blee
Crow	kanji	kahn jee
Hawk	cetan	chay dahn

HUMAN BODY

		Pronounced:
Hair	pehin	pay heen
Eyes	ista	ee shdah
Mouth	i	ee
Shoulder	ablo	ah blow
Back	cuwi	choo wee
Feet	si	see
Legs	huki	hoo kee
Hand	nape	nah pay
Arm	isto	ees doe
Head	nata	nah dah
Face	ite	ee day
Nose	pasu	pah soo

PEOPLE

		Pronounced:
Girl	wicin	wee-cheen
Boy	hoksila	hok-she-la
Woman	winyan	wee-yahn
Man	wicasa	wee-cha-sha
Baby	hoksicala	hok-she-cha-lah
Grandmother	unci	oon-chee
Grandfather	lala	lah-lah
Family	tiwahe	dee-wah-hay

Sign Language

Europeans began arriving in North America during the late 1490s. Anthropologists (scientists who study people and cultures) estimate that there were around 300 different Native American languages spoken in North America at that time. Sadly, many languages disappeared before they could be studied and understood. Today, only around 150 of these languages are still spoken. Their survival is threatened as elders pass away and native children do not learn their tribal language.

With so many different languages, how did tribes communicate? Sign language was a common means of communication for the people of the Great Plains. The Kiowa were renowned as excellent sign talkers. The Crow helped spread this sign language to other northern Plains tribes.

Buffalo

TRY THESE:

What is your name?

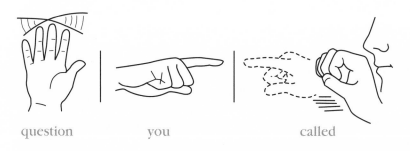

question   you   called

How old are you?

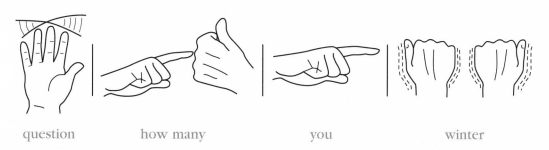

question   how many   you   winter

What do you do at camp?

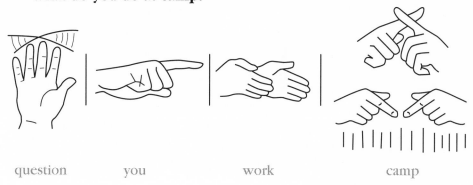

question   you   work   camp

I live here.

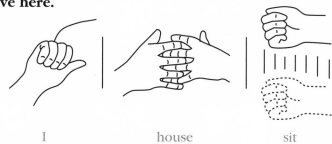

I   house   sit

SIGN LANGUAGE

I am going home.

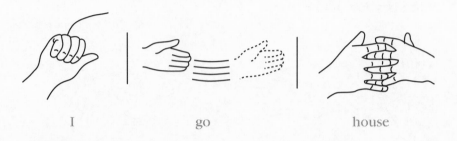

| I | go | house |

I am going to make camp.

| I | make | camp |

I build a fire.

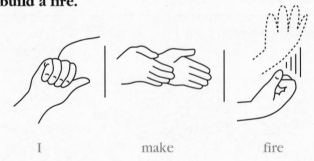

| I | make | fire |

Where is your horse?

| question | possession | horse |

Where do you live?

question	you	sit

Where is your home?

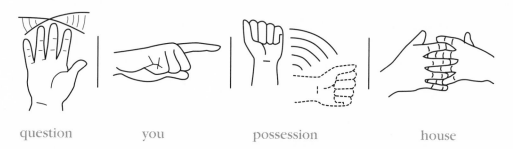

question	you	possession	house

I set up a tent.

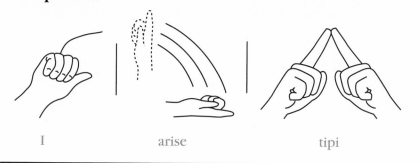

I	arise	tipi

I am hungry and want something to eat.

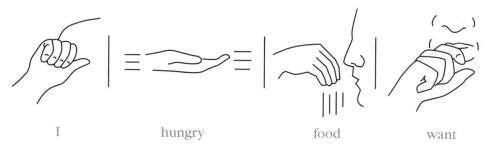

I	hungry	food	want

CAN YOU NAME THE STATES?

1. Named for the river which settlers named after a Native American tribe that inhabited the region at the time the first Europeans arrived. The name is believed to be a combination of two Choctaw words roughly meaning vegetation (*alba*) and gatherer (*amo*), which were applied to the Alabama, or *Alibamon*, people.

2. From the Aleut word for the Alaskan Peninsula, *alakhskhakh*.

3. From the Native American word *arizonac* believed to mean "place of the small spring."

4. Taken from the Arkansas River, which is named for the Native Americans of the Arkansa tribe.

5. From a Native American word, *Quinnehtukqut*, meaning "beside the long tidal river."

6. Named for the Illinois or *Illini*, a confederation of Native Americans of various tribes who inhabited Illinois and other sections of the Midwest at the time the first French explorers entered the region. The name Illinois is said to have been a French version of the Illini word for themselves, *Illiniwek*.

7. From the river which was named for the Iowa people, the Native Americans who lived in the region during early European exploration.

8. Named for the river that was named for the Kansa people, who once inhabited northeastern Kansas. The word Kansas means "people of the south wind."

9. From a Cherokee name for the area south of the Ohio River. The early pioneers spelled the name in many ways, including *Kaintuckee* and *Cantuckey*. Its meaning is disputed, but some historians believe it means "meadowland."

10. Taken from the name of an Algonquin village.

11. Named for one of the Great Lakes, Lake Michigan. The source of the lake name is disputed. Traditionally it is said to have been derived from the Algonquian term *michigama* meaning "big water" or "great lake." Others say the word comes from the Chippewa term *majigan*, meaning "clearing," which was given to an open area on the shores of the lake in the 17th century.

Language

12. From Sioux words for water (*mni*) and clear (*sota*)

13. From the words for big (*mitsi*) and river (*sitpi*) in an Algonquian language, probably Ojibwa or Cree.

14. Named after the Missouri River and is an Algonquian name for a group of people that lived near the mouth of the river.

15. From the Omaha name for the Platte River, *nibdhathka*, meaning "flat river."

16. The name Mexico has its source in the Central American Nahuatl language.

17. Named for the Dakota people who lived there. Residents chose to retain the name when the territory was divided into north and south states upon admission into the Union on November 2, 1889. This is the 39th state. The Dakota people are better known as the Eastern Sioux.

18. From the Ohio River, which forms the southern and southeastern and part of the eastern boundaries of the state. The word is thought to derive from an Iroquois word meaning either "great" or "beautiful" river.

19. From the Choctaw term for Indian Territory, which combined *okla*, meaning "people" or "nation," and *homa*, meaning "red."

20. From a Sioux term meaning "friends" or "allies." It was first applied to a United States territory in 1861. When South Dakota entered the Union on November 2, 1889, as the 40th state, its people chose to keep the name.

21. From the word *tanasi*, the Cherokee name for the Little Tennessee River.

22. From the southeast Native American Caddo word *tÇyóa¡* meaning friend.

23. From a Native American word meaning those who dwell high up or mountaintop dwellers.

24. Named after the Wisconsin River, which is derived from the French version of an Ojibwa term that may mean "gathering of the waters" or "place of the beaver."

Hunting
BEFORE THE HORSE

Whenever possible, the nomadic hunters worked together to trap an entire herd of buffalo. They often used a naturally formed box canyon. The Blackfeet were one of the first tribes to build a special pen for this purpose. The pen was called a piskin (pee-skeen), the word for corral in their language. The piskin was made from logs, which were stacked several feet high. The logs formed an oval large enough to hold around 100 buffalo. Sharp pointed stakes lined the inside wall, at the same height as a buffalo's ribs. This kept the animals from crashing through the walls to escape. The floor of the piskin was dug down almost two feet. This made it easy for the animals to gallop in, but much harder to escape.

Use of the piskin demanded careful planning and precise teamwork. The women and children of the tribe often helped the hunting party. Piles of brush were placed at intervals for miles out onto the prairie. Members of the tribe hid behind the piles, which formed an ever-smaller V-shape. A buffalo-robed decoy was often used to lure the herd into the mouth of the V. From behind the brush piles, the hunters made loud noises and tried to stampede the herd into the piskin. This was a very dangerous undertaking for the hunters.

Once the buffalo had entered the piskin, the entrance was sealed with a sturdy gate. Using bow and arrow or lances, the hunters killed the trapped animals. When this method was successful, it provided huge quantities of meat, which would feed the tribe for many weeks.

The hunters often stalked the herd to hunt individual animals. Hunting on foot was very dangerous, especially if an animal was only wounded. Buffalo are very nervous animals. Although their eyesight is poor, they have an excellent sense of both smell and hearing. The hunting party would approach the herd from downwind, covered in buffalo robes. The hunters crawled along the ground until they were 100–150 yards from the herd. At the signal they dropped their robes, shooting arrows into the herd with their longbows.

The longbow was a large weapon, up to six feet in length. It was designed to launch arrows a great distance. Special arrows, nearly five feet long, were fashioned by inserting lightweight reeds, one inside the other. The arrow tip was made from a bird bone, instead of stone. This also helped to keep the arrow lightweight, so it would travel farther.

When they were able to hunt from horseback, the horse became their most powerful weapon.

HEAD-SMASHED-IN BUFFALO

Today you can still visit an amazing piece of Native American history. When you travel to Alberta, Canada you will find a place where the foothills of the Rocky Mountains meet the Great Plains. Step back in time as you walk around the world's oldest, largest and best-preserved buffalo jump, which the nomads named Head-Smashed-In.

Bone and tool beds below the jump's sandstone cliffs grew to more than 30 feet thick during centuries of use. UNESCO (the United Nations Educational, Scientific and Cultural Organization) named Head-Smashed-In Buffalo Jump, a World Heritage Site in 1981. They ranked it with the pyramids of Egypt in historical importance. Native hunters first used Head-Smashed-In nearly 5,700 years ago. (More than 500 years before the first pyramid was built in Egypt!)

Head-Smashed-In is just one part of a huge kill site used by the nomadic hunters. Why did the hunters choose this site? The natural features of the landscape made it a perfect place to hunt buffalo on foot.

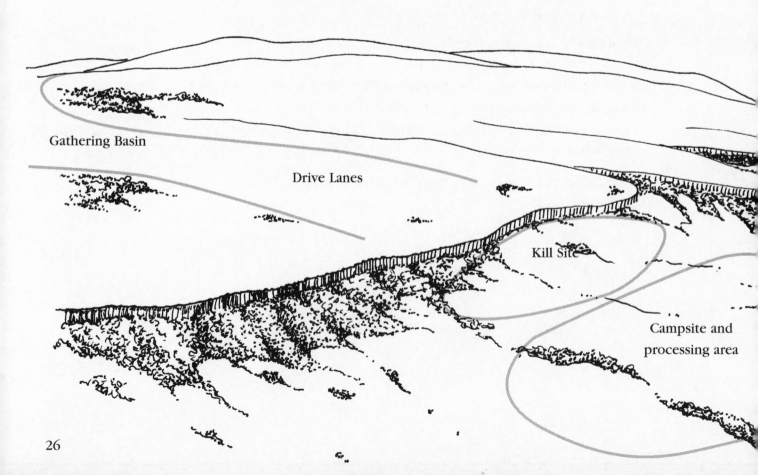

Gathering Basin

Drive Lanes

Kill Site

Campsite and processing area

JUMP

THE GATHERING BASIN

Look at the map. Find the Olsen Creek Basin. This is where the hunt began. The hunters lured the buffalo herds into the basin and sent them toward the "drive lanes."

DRIVE LANES

The Head-Smashed-In Buffalo Jump has a complex network of "drive lanes." These "drive lanes" were used to gather the buffalo herds, sending them toward the cliff.

KILL SITE

The actual "jump" was a cliff about 30 feet high and 300 feet wide. As the hunters stampeded the herd over the cliff, the buffalo fell to their deaths.

CAMP SITE

On the flat prairie next to the jump, the tribes made camp for days to process the meat and hides from the kill.

Parts of a Buffalo

In the fall, hunters were after the heavily furred buffalo hides. These made warm buffalo robes, bed coverings, winter lodge floors and tipi linings.

These heavy hides served as protection against the blizzard winds and deep snows that would soon follow. The summer hides were easily cleaned of their much thinner wool. They were used for tipis, saddlebags, regalia cases, travois skins and many other useful items.

Carved buffalo horn spoons
Ceremonial rattles made of rawhide
Buffalo rawhide pail

Hunting

USES FOR BUFFALO PARTS:

RAWHIDE:
Containers
Shields
Buckets
Moccasin Soles
Drums
Splints
Mortars
Cinches
Ropes
Sheaths
Saddles
Stirrups
Bull Boats
Masks
"Parfleche"
Ornaments
Lariats
Straps
Caps
Quirts
Snowshoes
Shrouds

**TANNED
BUFFALO HIDE:**
Moccasin Tops
Winter Robes
Bedding
Belts
Bags
Tipi Covers
Tipi Liners
Bridles
Backrests
Tapestries
Sweatlodge Covers

GALL STONES:
Yellow Paints

MEAT:
Immediate Use
Sausages
Cached Meat
Jerky (Dehydrated)
Pemmican (Processed)

HORNS:
Cups
Fire Carrier
Powderhorn
Spoons
Ladles
Headdresses
Signals
Toys
Medication

**HOOVES,
FEET &
DEWCLAWS:**
Glue
Rattles
Spoons

BEARD:
Ornamentations
Dolls

SKULL:
Sun Dance
Medicine Prayers
Other Rituals

BRAIN:
Hide Preparation

TEETH:
Ornamentation

TONGUE:
Choice Meat

BLADDER:
Pouches
Medicine Bags

TENDONS:
Sinews – Sewing
Bowstrings

MUSCLES:
Bows
Thread
Arrow Ties
Cinches

BLOOD:
Soups
Puddings

FAT:
Tallow
Soaps
Hair Grease
Cosmetic Aids

TAIL:
Medicine Switch
Fly Brush
Decorations
Whips

HAIR:
Headdresses
Pad Fillers
Pillows
Ropes
Ornaments
Hair Pieces
Halters
Bracelets
Medicine Balls
Moccasin Lining
Doll Stuffing

**PAUNCH
LINER:**
Wrappings (Meat)
Buckets
Collapsible Cups
Basins
Canteens

BONES:
Fleshing Tools
Pipes
Knives
Arrowheads
Shovels
Splints
Sleds
Saddle Trees
War Clubs
Scrapers
Quirts
Awls
Paintbrushes
Game Dice
Tableware
Toys
Jewelry

LIVER:
Tanning Agents

**STOMACH
CONTENTS:**
Medicines

**STOMACH
LINER:**
Water Containers
Cooking Vessels

CHIPS:
Fuel
Diaper Powder

Hunting RANGE OF THE AMERICAN BISON

The bison once covered most of North America. In less than 75 years, most were destroyed. The remaining few are in remote areas and a national park.

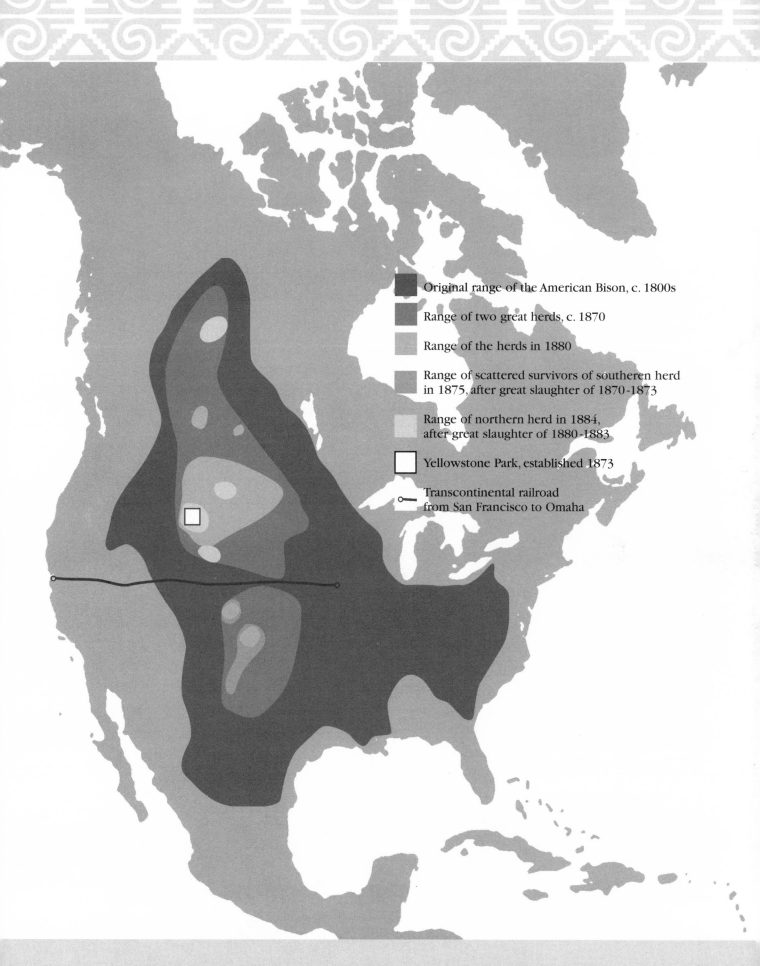

Original range of the American Bison, c. 1800s

Range of two great herds, c. 1870

Range of the herds in 1880

Range of scattered survivors of southeren herd in 1875, after great slaughter of 1870-1873

Range of northern herd in 1884, after great slaughter of 1880-1883

Yellowstone Park, established 1873

Transcontinental railroad from San Francisco to Omaha

The Horse
IN NORTH AMERICA

The Spanish explorer Coronado brought horses to North America on his ships in 1541. It was not the first time there had been horses on the Great Plains. The horse was coming home.

Eohippus

The horse originated on the North American continent nearly 60 million years ago. The oldest equine ancestor was called *Eohippus*, the Dawn Horse. The true horse we know today as *Equus callabus* lived on the Great Plains almost one million years ago.

No one can say exactly why the horse disappeared from North America. It happened about 10,000 years ago. It may have been a result of the Ice Age. But before the horse disappeared from North America altogether, a number of horses managed to migrate to Asia over the land bridge that connected the two continents at that time.

The presence of Europeans in North America had a great impact upon the native people of the Great Plains. The first instrument of change was the gun. The Spanish colony established in New Mexico forbade the trading of guns or horses to native people. Yet the Spaniards had the local Pueblo people work with their horses, and they began to acquire horsemanship skills. For nearly 100 years, only a few stray and stolen horses found their way into the hands of the Plains Indians.

In 1680 an uprising by the native Pueblo Indians drove the Spaniards out of the area temporarily. This left large herds of horses available for the Plains Indians. Among the earliest native people to take advantage of the horse were the Apache, living in the Arkansas Valley. The Apache traded regularly with the Pueblo, so they were able to acquire both horses and horsemanship techniques.

Through stealing and intertribal trading, horses quickly spread across the Great Plains. By the 1700s, both the Pawnee and the Wichita had horses. By 1750, the Blackfeet in Canada were fully mounted. By 1770, the horse reached the Sioux in western Minnesota. These native peoples rode their mounts with such skill and ease, Europeans were convinced that they must have been riding for centuries.

The horse transformed the nomads of the Great Plains into culture of great abundance. Hunters could now pursue the buffalo on horseback. This allowed them to hunt farther from the camp and more effectively than on foot. Horses permitted 2–3 mounted hunters to kill enough buffalo to provide meat to feed an extended family for a week.

With the horse replacing the dog as a pack animal, other things changed for the Plains tribes. A horse could pull a travois of 300 pounds. This allowed the nomads to carry larger supplies of food and retain more personal possessions. Tipis were also larger because the horse travois was made with much longer poles. The horse helped the tribe move as much as 40 miles each day. Because of its importance as a pack animal, the horse was called `Sunka Tanka (shoon-kah tahn-kah), meaning Big Dog or Great Dog.

The wide sea of prairie grass provided a constant food supply for their horses. With this new prosperity, both the horse population and the human population increased. Intertribal trading grew and flourished. Life had never been so good on the Great Plains.

The Horse

Unfortunately, the introduction of the horse also became a major reason for conflict for the Plains Indians. The combination of the horse and the recent acquisition of guns made buffalo hunting easier than it had ever been. Because food was more abundant, the hunters had much more free time. Hunters used this newly found freedom to plan, make, and celebrate warfare. Raids against other peoples would often bring more horses into the tribe. The horse became an important symbol of wealth. Stealing a horse from another tribe was considered an honorable activity.

The Horse
BLOOD BROTHER

Long ago, my ancestors first gazed upon this great beast. We named him `Sunka Tanka (The Great Dog). Other men called him horse. Once we climbed upon his strong back, our lives were forever changed.

His beauty captivated us. His intelligence inspired us. His athletic ability amazed us. We were then touched by his spirit, his keen sensitivity, overwhelming loyalty and purity of heart. The Indian and the horse established a bond of brotherhood. As the Europeans struggled to tame the American West, the Indian struggled to keep his hunting ground and home.

If not for the horse, the Plains Indians would never have survived the invasion of the Europeans. With the horse came the Golden Era of the Horse, changing the lives of the Buffalo People forever. Horses were much more than beasts of burden to the Plains Indians. The special relationship between Indians and their horses was based upon trust, loyalty and respect. European settlers watched with amazement, as the Plains Indians became one of the world's greatest horse cultures.

The lifelong partnership between a Plains Indian and a horse began at an early age. An infant traveled in a baby cradle attached securely to it's mother's saddle. The great animal's strength and rhythm gently rocked the baby to sleep. Young children helped care for their family's horses. They helped make horse equipment, watched horses in training, learned and practiced riding. Plains Indian children were accomplished riders by the time they were 12. All horsemanship skills were learned by both boys and girls. These skills were especially important for the young boys. They were destined to be the next generation of buffalo hunters and warriors.

A horse was not only reliable transportation for the Plains Indians. He was an ally on the hunt and a trusted comrade in battle. A horse trained for the buffalo hunt was not used for any other purpose. This animal was a hunter's most prized possession. A buffalo horse or "runner" was typically a young horse, around four years old. The chosen horse was at the peak of its speed and stamina. The runner needed the ability to sprint over both long and short distances. He also needed the intelligence to learn quickly and respond to subtle commands. Imagine the courage required maneuvering through a panicked herd of stampeding buffalo, facing an animal as huge and fierce as the buffalo without shying away.

The runner was carefully trained and pampered. He was fed the finest of grasses. During the hot summer months, he was bathed in cool water. During the cold winter months he was warmed with buffalo robes. While the other horses grazed peacefully near the outskirts of the camp, the runner was tethered next to its owner's tipi in the heart of the encampment. Here the runner was in danger from only the boldest of horse raiders. Runners shared their pampered lives with horses used on the battle field.

Family &

The horse brought great changes and ushered in the golden years of the Buffalo People of the Great Plains. Throughout, their history, one thing remained constant. The Plains Indians were completely devoted to the family unit and clan. The family was the most treasured possession of all.

Plains tribes developed communities that encouraged unity and harmony. They created an elaborate system of rules and behavior to reduce conflict within the tribe. Enforcement of this code was necessary for the survival of the family. The land was unforgiving, the climate harsh, and the resources scarce. In order to survive, the people lived in small, self-reliant, nomadic bands for much of the year. Everyone, from the oldest to the youngest, had a position and role within the great, extended family. The fate of each individual depended on the actions of the entire tribe. The well being of the tribe rested on the actions of each individual member.

Parents, children, grandparents, aunts and uncles, lived and camped together. Men hunted together. Upon the hunters return to the campsite, women worked together to process the meat and hides and prepare meals. Elders passed their experience and knowledge to the young. In turn, the young looked after their aging relatives.

Clan

These large, extended families were part of even larger groups called clans. Clans were the basic unit of social organization on the Great Plains. Members were required to protect fellow clansmen in battle and take responsibility for the misdeeds or crimes of other clan members.

The Crow referred to the clan concept with a phrase "as driftwood lodges." Just as pieces of driftwood come together in the raging waters of a river or stream, so too, families join in clans to travel life's dangerous journeys. This concept refers to spiritual rather than a physical journey, for the family units of a clan did not always live or travel together. Most clans were too large for such an arrangement to be practical.

Many plains clans had colorful or humorous nicknames. Crow clans, for example, included the "Filth Eaters," the "Bad War Deeds," and the "Greasy Inside the Mouths." Among the Sioux, were clans named "Wears a Dogskin Around the Neck," "Breakers of the Law," and "Not Burdened with Many Possessions." Other clans took their names from physical traits. For example, one Cheyenne family was called "Narrow Nose Bridge," because the family members had close-set eyes. Still other clans bore the names of animals or remarkable people, places, or events. The Mandan had the "Badger" and "Speckled Eagle" clans, while the Omaha boasted the "Wind" and "Deer" clans.

In addition to the family and clan unit, plains nomads also developed strong ties to a hunting community or band. A band consisted of men from several clans. It was large enough to provide protection from enemy tribes, yet small enough to assure proper supplies of food during harsh, prairie winters. Members shared food and other resources and bore responsibility for the safety of the band. They were always free to visit or join other bands.

The band was a united political and economic group, but did not formally appoint chiefs. The older, more experienced men of the band provided leadership. These men were known for their wisdom, generosity, and skill at settling disputes.

Each summer, the bands that composed the tribe came together for a few weeks. They gathered at an agreed upon site to visit, trade goods, hold counsel meetings, and conduct important ceremonies.

Like clans, bands had nicknames. The Cheyenne "Scabby Hand" band was named after a leader who had a skin disorder. The "White Wolf" band was named after its founder, a man said to be as crafty and ill tempered as a wolf. Others bands were named after the regions in which they camped. Unlike clan names that could be traced back for generations, band names changed often. This clearly showed the constant shift in structure and character of the hunting communities.

Clan

A WOMAN'S WAY

When the European explorers saw that Indian women did much of the physical labor within the tribe, they incorrectly assumed that Native Americans considered women to be inferior. What the Europeans did not understand, was that by performing tasks essential to the survival of the family and the tribe, Indian women existed as equals with their men.

Women's work was highly valued in Native American society. Women made clothing, collected the daily store of firewood and water, prepared meals and processed her husband's kills. Doing these tasks well brought women honor and prestige within the tribe. Women often made most of the decisions regarding the family household, including the location for the tipi itself. Among many Native American societies, women not only ran the household, but also owned the tipi itself and all of its contents. The more skilled a woman at managing her household, the more social and economic power she gained. Native American family life was not a matter of one sex having power over another. Instead, it was a relationship of mutual interdependence and respect.

Among my ancestors, the Sioux, women were valued for their skills in crafting material goods. Women tallied their domestic accomplishments in much the same way men counted their war deeds. Dots carved along the elk horn handles of tools recorded tanning and completed tipis. A black dot represented one tanned buffalo hide. Red dots were completed tipis. Sioux women also held contests in which they exhibited their prize moccasins, dresses, storage bags, and even baby cradles. Those who specialized in making cradles, rawhide containers, and sewing together and decorating tipis, discovered their skills were a source of wealth. Many were hired and paid for their skills by other, less skilled women.

The portable shelter for all seasons was the tipi, a tent that evolved over the centuries into the ideal shelter for a nomad on the Great Plains. The word "tipi" comes from two Sioux words that mean "used to dwell in." Other tribes used to call it a lodge, and the poles that held it up were called lodgepoles.

With a thin covering of buffalo hide, the tipi remained cool in the sweltering summer heat. Insulating dew cloths made it snug during the cold winters. Best of all, a tipi could be quickly dismantled and easily transported when they moved to follow the buffalo. The tipi was more than just protection from the elements. The tent was a sanctified place. The circular floorplan symbolized the shape of the earth. The floor represented the earth itself and the walls were the sky. The poles were pathways to the Great Spirit, living on high.

Most Plains tribeswomen made their own tipi and bore the responsibility for it. Making a tipi was an enormous task. First, a woman would strip the bark from the lodge poles. Then she skinned as many as 14 buffalo and tanned the hides. Next she sewed them together to make the tipi covering. Finally, she selected the exact spot upon which to erect the tipi. Two women working together could erect a tipi in about an hour.

Women

Once a tipi cover was beyond repair, it was cut apart and recycled. The portion of the tipi cover at the top was filled with smoke and ashes and was waterproof. This hide was an excellent choice for making moccasins.

When the time came to strike camp, women dismantled and folded the tipis and attached them to the A-shaped travois, using the lodge poles themselves which was pulled by a horse. The long wooden poles were a precious possession on the largely treeless Great Plains. Five lodge poles were equal to the value of one horse.

Young girls were taught horsemanship skills, because women had a similar bond with horses as the men of the tribe. Women were responsible for moving all their worldly belongings to follow the buffalo herds. Women relied upon their horses to make this possible. They entrusted their lives and the lives of their children to their faithful beasts of burden.

Unlike the spirited warhorses and speedy buffalo runners, women's horses were mainly pack animals. Women's horses were sturdy and calm, with gentle dispositions. These horses were able to travel great distances with a minimum of food or water.

A woman's horse equipment was decorated with intricate beadwork, horsehair, brass cones and bells, trade cloth, shells and coins. These pieces were truly works of art. This handmade tack not only honored her faithful beast of burden, it demonstrated her artistic talent and industrious nature to the rest of the tribe. Every family possession was carefully packed in its proper place for the 15–20 mile daily trek.

Traditionally, Native Americans did not use saddles. Occasionally a Spanish-made saddle was acquired through trade. Some Plains tribes constructed a primitive wooden saddle, used only by women. Nicknamed "Crow saddles," they were very decorative and probably extremely uncomfortable. The Crow saddle had extremely large horns in both front and back, often decorated with elaborate beadwork. Most women preferred to ride on a large elkhide or buffalo hide pad, secured with a rawhide girth. Rawhide lacing was used to attach additional gear to the pad.

The highly decorated crupper extended from the hide saddle down the back and across the rump. It was only for decoration, but it did help protect the horse from insects and the harsh sun.

Women used simple braided buffalo or horsehair bitless bridles with their mounts. Attached to the browband was a decoration called a keyhole. One look at its shape and you can see how it got this name. The keyhole was beaded and often had dyed horsehair trim. Women also placed decorative horse collars or martingales around their horses' necks. The collar was only for decoration, boasting elaborate beadwork in traditional family colors and patterns.

45

Beaded saddlebags in the shape of large envelopes were placed across the horse's back. Household items were stored in these bags, which were often decorated with long fringe. The movement of the fringe helped keep the flies away from the horse's back legs while traveling.

They also carried bags called "possible bags" because they could contain possibly anything. They had many different styles and shapes. Some were made from furred animal skins. Others were made from tanned hide and decorated with abstract patterns of glass beads and quillwork. A common container, the rawhide parfletch, so called from the French phrase "par un fletch," which meant "to turn an arrow," was an envelope pattern that was etched and painted in geometric design. Possible bags were attached to a woman's hide saddle while traveling. Later, they were neatly hung on the inner wall of the tipi, several feet off the ground to discourage wild animals attracted by the food.

The women rode as they traveled each day. Children too small to ride a horse would sit on the travois. An infant was secured in a baby cradle, which hung from the hide pad over the horse's right front leg. When she was riding, this arrangement made it much easier for a mother to care for her infant. Picture the parade of horses in colorfully beaded regalia, pulling travois covered with brightly decorated possible bags, jingling hawk bells and brass cones, mixed with the sounds of children's laughter and song.

Project
POSSIBLE BAG

Plains Indian women called them "possible" bags, because they could hold possibly anything. They were used to carry household items as they traveled and were hung on walls of the tipi when camping.

ITEMS NEEDED:

fabric at least 36 inches wide
> (cloth, felt, leather, artificial fur)

10 yards of leather lacing or yarn

100 pony beads (assorted colors)

large upholstery needle

INSTRUCTIONS:

1. Cut a rectangle of fabric 12 inches wide and 36 inches long.

2. Lay the fabric on a flat surface with the short sides at the top and bottom of the rectangle.

3. Bring the bottom edge of the fabric up and fold so that it lays 8 inches from the top edge.

4. Stitch the two sides of the pouch together using the large needle and yarn or leather lacing.

5. Fold the top edge of the rectangle over the top of the pouch.

6. Cut a strip of fabric 1-inch wide by 36 inches long. Attach this as the carrying strap of the pouch.

7. Decorate your possible bag with beads and fringe.

Among the Plains Indian tribes, both sexes depended upon one another for survival. Both sexes had to earn the right to marry. A girl who reached adolescence usually married quickly. She proved her worthiness by demonstrating her good homemaking skills and mastery of crafts. The marital age for men varied from tribe to tribe. Some married in their late teens or early twenties. Others waited until they were older. A man usually postponed the responsibilities of a family until he had proven his manhood. He would have to demonstrate success on the warpath and the hunt before taking a wife.

Courtship began with the attempts of a young man to secure a girl's affection. Young men and women were not permitted to openly associate with one another. A suitor had to be discreet when attracting the attention of the girl he wished to wed. It usually started with brief conversations in public. For these occasions, he would don his finest clothing and carefully groom his hair so as to appear fresh and pure. Other times, he might wait patiently along a path near the young girl's home, hoping to meet her as she went to get water or wood. If she

were carrying water, he would offer to assist her and at the same time hold her hand. Berry gathering offered yet another way for the couple to share moments together. Any opportunity to prove his worthiness and win the heart of his beloved was welcomed.

Marriage

Female attraction to beautiful music was an important factor of courtship on the plains. Men serenaded young women with courting flutes. These slender instruments were carefully crafted by shamans who often carved into them images of animals associated with love and passion. Each flute was accompanied by a magical love song that the shaman composed according to instructions he received in a vision.

A suitor played the flute in order to attract a girl's attention and to let her know that he wanted to talk to her. The flute's melodic sound would entice the young woman to leave her tipi and search for the musician playing the entrancing love song.

To further increase their powers of persuasion, suitors could enlist the aid of an "Elk Dreamer." This particular shaman was a specialist in the affairs of the heart. It was believed that he obtained his supernatural powers from the bull elk. Among the Plains people, this animal was considered to be the symbol of power and love. The Elk Dreamer would carefully make courting medicine and love potions that would insure success in love. Potions placed in deerskin pouches and hand crafted love charms were supplied to serious suitors for a price. When in the presence of their love interests, young men would wear these magical items around their necks.

A courting couple could rarely escape the watchful stares of grand-parents or the curiosity of young children. In order to shield their encounters from prying eyes and obtain privacy, suitors enveloped themselves and their intended brides in blankets. This custom of "standing wrapped in a blanket" enabled lovers to hide their faces from passersby and talk in private. It was customary never to inter-rupt a young couple covered by a courting blanket.

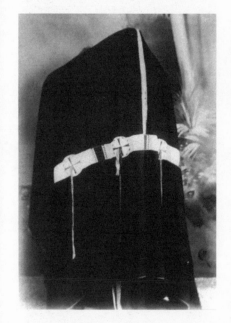

A young man's older sister often made the highly prized courting blanket. Approaching a woman with a blanket was a sign of serious marital intent. A very popular Indian girl might find a line of young men outside her tipi with blankets over their arms. Customs required that she give each one a chance. But she could decline to huddle with a man, or cut his time short, in favor of a more attractive suitor.

Marriage proposals varied among the tribes of the Great Plains. One way involved an agreement with the girl's parents permitting the future groom to live with the family for a period of one year. During this time, the young man had to prove that he could be a good provider and protector. The girl also had to show her potential husband that she was an excellent homemaker. After the trial period, if the arrangement was pleasing to the parents, the couple would marry in a public feast.

Courtship &

Among other tribes, when a young man felt confident of a favorable reception, he enlisted his brother or a close friend to offer a formal proposal of marriage to his intended's male relatives. A girl could turn down any man she deemed unappealing. If she found her suitor acceptable, an agreement on the bride price would be negotiated. As generous a gift in horses, food, and other goods as the groom could afford would be offered to the girl's family. In no way were these seen as direct payment for a wife. Such gifts clearly showed a man's potential as a provider and his understanding of the woman's value to her family.

Once a marriage proposal was made and the bride price established and delivered, the young woman's male relatives would meet in her father's tipi to discuss the pros and cons of the union. If they rejected the offer, the gifts were returned. If they accepted, the gifts were distributed among family members. The young bride-to-be would be dressed in her finest deerskin outfit. Gifts were collected equal to the value of those given by the boy's family. Both girl and gifts were sent off to the home of her future husband, and a marriage feast followed. When the celebration ended, the groom would escort his bride home to their new tipi. It was often a wedding gift made by other women in the tribe.

Marriage

In some instances her family arranged a young woman's marriage. Girls had the right to refuse their parent's choice, but this was rare. Marriage, in some tribes, was not expected to be a love match. It was considered a social contract for sharing economic responsibilities and child rearing. Young women were frequently married to older men with tribal status who could ensure her material well-being. They were not expected to have emotional relationships with their husbands. Instead they made strong bonds with their children, relatives, clan members, and other women in the community. If they were not compatible with their husbands, Indian women could easily divorce. A woman who was living with her husband's family separated from him by simply gathering up her belongings and small children and returning home to her parents. If a woman made the tipi in which the couple lived, she was sole owner of the home and all its contents. To divorce her husband, she placed all of his possessions outside and told him to leave.

As an indirect result of the acquisition of the horse, marriage customs changed among the Plains Indians. For centuries, men usually only took one wife. In earlier years, a skilled homemaker could butcher as many as three buffalo per day. When the Plains tribes were fully mounted, hunters became more efficient, bringing home nearly fourteen thousand pounds of buffalo meat and hides to be processed from a single hunt. Even the most industrious woman could not keep up with this monumental amount of work. It became common practice for a man to take two or more wives. In addition, the death rate among men was much higher, because of the dangers of the hunt, horse raids, and warfare. There were often more women than men in any given tribe. Young women, widows and their children, all needed husbands to provide for them.

Marriage

When a man married the older sister of a family, he was entitled to marry the younger ones as they came of age. These marriages usually required no ceremony. The two families were already considered bonded. The man simply gave his father-in-law a new horse, and the younger sister moved into his home. Many wives welcomed this arrangement. The work load was shared and her sisters provided constant companionship.

If a man had two or more wives who were not related, separate households were established. This ensured the proper amount of living space for each family and prevented any conflict between wives. The first wife retained a position of honor, supervised all the work, and had special privileges.

Providing for a large family consisting of many wives and children was a source of great pride for a man, but it was also hard work.

55

Childhood
BIRTH AND INFANCY

When a wife was having her first baby, it was customary in many plains tribes for the husband to leave the village and go hunting. Sometimes he might stay with his father's people until the baby was born. The wife was left in the care of her own female relatives, or an older woman. Since all the plains tribes were nomadic, babies were often born on the trail. Whenever possible, suitable preparations were made for such births.

The newborn's umbilical cord represented a connection to both family and tribe. Because of its great importance, it was placed inside an elaborately beaded pouch. Girl's pouches took the form of turtles. Boys were made in the shape of snakes or lizards. In infancy, the pouch was attached to the baby's clothing or cradle as a longevity charm. When the child grew too large for the cradle, the pouch was worn around the neck for spiritual protection and was thought to guide the child's behavior. The Cheyenne people believed that a child who was restless was looking for a misplaced umbilical pouch. The Arapaho were convinced that a child would surly die if this pouch was lost.

Infants raised in mild climates spent much of their time in cradleboards. These boards were padded with moss or shredded bark. Safe inside the snug device, the baby could easily be hoisted on its mother's back or set upright under the shade of a tree while mother performed her chores.

Cradleboards were objects of great beauty. They were painstakingly made from wood, tanned animal skins, and canvas. They were elaborately decorated with beadwork, porcupine quills, brass tacks, and symbolic paintings. A cradle was crafted by a small group of women. These craftswomen would present it to a new mother in a special ceremony held just after the birth of the child. Before the baby was placed inside, the hood of the cradle was smudged with incense. The chief cradle-maker prayed that the child would enjoy a long life. Then the baby was tied into its new bed. For the next six to seven months, it accompanied its mother throughout the day. If mother walked, the cradleboard and baby were strapped to her back. If she rode horseback, it was hung on the saddle. Once the cradleboard was outgrown, it was dismantled during the course of a special ceremony.

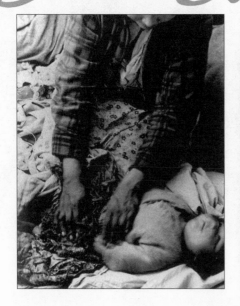  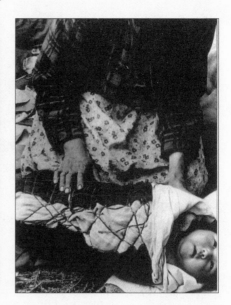

Diapers were made from a variety of organic materials. My people, the Sioux, used soft, packed down plucked from cattails. This down was tucked around the baby's bottom. Other tribes made diapers from the soft, inner bark of willow trees, or used certain types of moss. This material was rolled into balls, then layered around the baby's body.

To prevent chafing of the skin within the diapers, babies were powdered from the waist down with aged, finely ground buffalo manure. Diaper material was held in place by a soft cloth or blanket secured with leather thongs. Whenever possible, diapers were changed each time they were soiled, then washed, air-dried, and reused.

Indian mothers relied on many organic salves and medicines to soothe their infants' ailments. For one of the most common problems, diaper rash, they mixed grease with red clay. Even today, Indian women regard this ointment as better than most store remedies. A mother might give her baby a bit of gristle on which to chew if it suffered from teething pain. If that failed, she would catch a mouse, roast it, and rub the meat over the child's throbbing gums. Stomach distress could be treated with the finely ground crop of a wild turkey, mixed with water.

NAMES

Infants became recognized members of their community at a naming ceremony, usually held after birth. Before this ceremony, an infant really didn't have a human identity. Babies who were still born or who died prior to the naming ceremony were neither mourned nor given burial rites. They were still considered to be part of the spirit world.

Since it was believed to influence a child's destiny, a baby's name was carefully selected. Being chosen to name a child was a great honor in every plains tribe. Grandparents, renowned warriors, or tribal medicine men were often asked to name boys. Older women with perfect morals were frequently asked to name girls. Names usually revealed the child's gender, either by a suffix attached to the word or phrase or by the subject matter. Girls were often named for flowers and songbirds, while boys were named for predatory animals and birds.

Little Feather

Otter

Fast Turtle

Low Flying Eagle Woman

Little Foot

Black Hawk

Big Mountain

Many Arrows

Laughing Crow

Kicking Bird

Red Cloud

Grey Wolf

Sioux boys were generally named after their oldest living relative. If those names had been taken by an older brother, they would be named after the warlike deeds or accomplishments of their father. For the Cheyenne, dreams, unusual animals, or memorable experiences inspired names. One Cheyenne brave, who had seen a turtle while fishing, named a baby boy, "White Turtle." While gathering firewood, an aging Cheyenne woman encountered an unusually marked bird, and she later named a female infant, "Red Wing."

Among the Plains tribes, female children usually kept their names for life. However, their parents or siblings might hold a renaming ceremony, if the girl became sick or suffered other misfortune. The new name was thought to bring better luck.

Lame Deer

Standing Bear

A boy received new names throughout his teens and well into manhood. As he matured, these names reflected his changing status. For example, a boy might have been given the name "Red Fox" during his naming ceremony. As a teen, an arrow struck and severely wounded his right arm during a surprise enemy attack. He might then take the new name of "Strong Right Arm," because he survived his wounds from his first brush with death. A great horse raider named himself "Many White Horses," because he stole only white horses from hostile neighbors. Once a man had returned from his first successful war expedition, he would earn a final name. This final name could reflect a great act of bravery, an actual event on the battlefield, or another significant accomplishment. This was important if the man chose to begin courting a young woman.

Buffalo Calf Woman

SPOTTED EAGLE

Last Horse

Red Wing

Lone Elk

Two Ponies

Childhood

FAMILY RELATIONSHIPS

Relationships between Plains children and their families were very close. It was impossible for an Indian child to become an orphan. This was due to a complex system of kinship. For instance, a male child called his father's brothers "Father," and his father's sisters, "Aunt." His mother's sisters were also his mothers, but her brothers were his uncles. Additionally, the child's circle of brothers and sisters included his father's brother's children. Even a child who lost both parents was absorbed into another part of its family.

Interactions between children were mostly friendly. Indian children seldom showed temper, jealousy, or resentment. If two boys were competing in a wrestling match, they would be encouraged by the shouts of parents and onlookers. Each boy would try to do his best. When one was thrown, the spectators would raise a great shout of laughter to show their enjoyment of the contest. As a result, youngsters emerged from these contests with laughter. Both boys were praised for a job well done and learned to accept both defeat and success. The importance of living on good terms with their fellows was drilled into children's heads from infancy.

Brothers and sisters enjoyed strong kinship bonds. As youngsters, they played the same game of "House" that modern children play. In this elaborate game, children imitated adult behavior, from setting up camp to buffalo hunting. The close relationship between brothers and sisters changed as they neared adolescence. Brothers took on the role of their sister's protector. Sisters began to make clothes and moccasins for their brothers. Their close daily interaction came to a close. Grown-up brothers and sisters were not permitted to look directly at one another. They could not speak directly to each other. Conversations took place by the use of go-betweens. A brother could not remain with his sister alone in a tipi. It would show her great disrespect, if he did.

Nonetheless, brothers and sisters remained close throughout their lives. Adult brothers would bring their sisters fresh meat from a buffalo hunt and gifts of fine horses from successful horse raids. To raise his status among his peers, sisters would make fine articles for their brothers to wear and carry. When brothers were killed in combat, it was the sister who led the mourning ceremony. Sometimes, sisters even followed brothers into battle. They would prepare meals for their warrior brothers and tend to any wounds they may suffer. Stories have been told among the Plains tribes of sisters who have even saved their brothers lives on the battlefield. A Cheyenne elder, named Buffalo Hump, spoke of a girl who saved her brother's life after his horse was shot from under him. Buffalo Calf Road Woman defended her brother in a similar situation and was honored by having the battle in which she fought named for her.

In contrast to the tremendous respect displayed between grown brothers and sisters, cousins and in-laws treated each other very differently. They were called "Iwatkusua," a Plains Indian term for "joking relatives." They mocked and teased each other constantly, embarrassing each other in public. A man might be teased for wearing dirty clothes or failing at the hunt. A woman might be mocked for her laziness or unattractive appearance. An outsider might consider these comments rude, but they were tolerated and indulged when the source was a jesting relative. Iwatkusua also played practical jokes. Some pranks were small, like stealing a saddlebag or other personal item. Others were more serious, like cutting someone's hair. Most of the time, a severe joke was followed up with a gift and plea for forgiveness.

These joking relationships served practical purposes within the Plains society. They created an acceptable manner to show public disapproval and disfavor. If someone acted improperly or violated social standards, who better to discipline them than a family member? This relationship enjoyed between humorous in-laws could also ease the way for possible future marriages.

Status

In some Plains tribes, like the Blackfoot, children of famous men enjoyed special treatment. The Blackfoot called these fortunate children "minipoka," or outstanding children. Usually this adored child of a wealthy family was pampered with praise and elaborate gifts from friends and family members. These gifts might include miniature tipis, toys, fancy clothes, and intricately beaded moccasins. As an adult, a minipoka was expected to assume an important role in the tribal community.

This concept of inherited status was rare, however. For most tribes, status was neither passed down nor fixed for life. Individuals earned a good name as a result of their actions and character. This meant that anyone could seek a position of honor within the tribe. The oral histories of the Buffalo People are filled with tales of unlikely youths who rose to leadership through their skills and good deeds.

One of the most popular of these stories involves an orphan boy. When he was very young, he was adopted by a poor, old woman. Too proud to ask for help, the little family would pitch their weather-beaten tipi on the outskirts of the camp. They did not want to expose their poverty; for fear that it would offend the entire community.

The boy asked the old woman to make him a bow and some arrows. They would enable him to provide food for her and repay her years of kindness. The weapons she made were magical and had supernatural powers. They permitted the boy to kill each animal he hunted with a single shot. Soon, he and his elderly companion were enjoying an abundance of food. In times of scarcity, the boy helped the rest of the tribe by providing huge quantities of meat using his magical bow and arrows. He grew up to become a respected tribal leader.

In early childhood, parents stressed the importance of generosity. It was key to raising one's status within the tribal community. Wealth on the Great Plains was not measured by how much one owned, but by how much one gave away. The more generosity a man or woman displayed, the more prestige he or she won. For example, the mere possession of many horses might be envied, but not admired. To be admired for his horses, a man had to have shown bravery in obtaining them. If he had stolen them from an enemy, it was very praiseworthy. Only by lending the horses or giving away the horses to less fortunate families, would a man raise his status and experience true respect and admiration from the entire tribe.

DISCIPLINE

According to tribal wisdom, the first ten years of life were critical to a person's development. Because of this, children were given considerable freedom. They were encouraged to experiment. Mistakes were viewed as part of the learning process, and were seldom punished.

Youngsters were thought to be close to the Spirit World. Their spirits were delicate, and so they must be treated with tolerance. If not, it was believed they might die. Therefore, most Native Americans used a gentle brand of discipline. Harsh words and spanking were avoided. They could upset a child's fragile soul. Parents used love and reason to handle problem behavior. If a child was misbehaving, it was simply asked to stop.

Only a few Plains tribes used a harsher form of discipline. The Blackfoot and the Crow were known for this. They used water to correct misbehavior. If a child cried too long, they would put it on it's back and pour water up it's nose. Older children, especially boys, might have water thrown directly into their faces. The water punishment was believed to be a very important toughening process that would prepare boys to become warriors. Before long, the warning words, "Bring the water!" would be enough to calm any rowdy child.

The Apache also relied on strong corrective measures. Like the Crow and Blackfoot, they placed great value on strength and courage. A small boy who misbehaved might be punished by having a hole punched in his earlobe by a needle-sharp awl. The Apache also used whipping as a means to keep children in line. Apache grandparents shared the responsibility for shaping a youngster's values and behavior. They, not the parents, administered physical punishment. Apache children often feared their grandparents, but ultimately had great respect for them.

Childhood

EDUCATION

Education of Native American children began early. Most of the training they would need as adults was acquired during the first ten years of their lives. Typically, their education focused on the skills related to their gender. Learning well by playing games could mean the difference between life and death as adults.

Boys followed in the footsteps of their fathers, uncles, and brothers. A Plains Indian father would craft miniature bows, arrows, and quivers for his son's use. He would carefully instruct him on the tracking of small game. A boy might go on his first hunting trip under the watchful eye of his grandfather. When he returned to camp, he presented his first kill to the grandfather or another elder, and asked for prayers to make him brave. Uncles often sang songs of celebration to honor these early achievements.

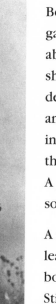

Boys had a great deal of freedom. They played games that stressed endurance, strength, and the ability to withstand pain. Their toys were slingshots, stilts, darts, and tops. Any toy that would develop the speed and agility needed for hunting and warfare was encouraged. Warrior dolls, dressed in full regalia, were given to boys. They impressed the importance of warrior life and proper dress. A pony was a necessity. A boy was gifted a pony as soon as he could sit on one's back.

A few boys in each community followed a spiritual leader rather than taking the road of war. These boys had inherited their rights as spiritual leaders. Still, they had to pass many tests designed to weed out the unfit. These trials included restricting their diet and freedom within the community.

A boy who chose the spiritual path was assigned to a shaman, or priest, around the age of nine. The shaman would teach the sacred law to his new student. The student would be subjected to difficult physical tests. At the end of a boy's training, his worthiness for a holy calling would be measured. The shaman did this by examining a piece of quartz or other crystal.

Indians were permissive with their daughters, as well as their sons. However, the rearing of little girls was different. This included teaching young girls a different pattern of speech and behavior. Despite these gender differences, girls were brought up very much the same way in every Native American culture.

The bond between a mother and daughter was very close. A daughter accompanied her mother everywhere. She learned what was expected of a woman by watching her mother. She picked berries and other useful plants. She helped to clean, gather wood, prepare hides, sew, quill, bead, cook, and manage the household. Girls also cared for younger children. Even at age six, a girl might have to feed, change, and amuse her siblings.

Each young girl's efforts were celebrated. When she began picking berries, the girl gave them to a female elder. This woman prayed that the child might lead a long life and have many healthy babies. Parents would display beadwork, possible bags, and moccasins made by their daughters on blankets nearby the tipi to be admired by those who passed by.

Fathers and brothers praised a little girl's efforts, as well. They wished her to develop her skills. When the girl reached ten, most of the household chores became hers alone.

Childhood

Girls also shared the games that boys played. Young girls lead active and unconfined lives. They were taught to ride and develop horsemanship skills. They joined their male companions in spirited ball games, relay races, diving for stones, capturing frogs, and stalking small game. Rough-housing was popular, and girls held war games with and against the boys.

Most of the games played by girls developed her domestic skills. Make-believe was especially popular. Little girls would imitate ways and customs of adults. Mothers made rag dolls representing women, boys, girls, and babies. The youngsters would invent ponies for their dolls using forks and sticks. They would mount the dolls on these ponies and pretend to move camp. Sometimes a doll family would have a wedding or a new baby would be born. Anything an adult would do was imitated.

Indian girls were encouraged to be physically active throughout their childhood. Exercise promoted grace and beauty. It built the strength needed for hard work and child-bearing. As a girl approached the age of eleven, the focus of her activities shifted. The pampering of early years began to take a back seat to adult responsibilities. She was made to run to the top of a hill without stopping. This was intended to improve her lungs and wind. Sometimes she carried all the water to and from the tipi. Pouting and complaints would only make the matter worse. She would then be instructed to run as she gathered the family's water. She was also limited to the amount of time she could spend with her male companions and her pony.

Storytelling, in addition to games, was a favored means of instruction for Native American children. By telling stories, adults continually reinforced tribal values, customs, and manners. They taught the young ones about nature, their history, and the people who influenced it.

On certain evenings throughout the year, the elders would hold court around the campfire. Children were encouraged to listen to the stories they told. These ranged from simple tales of everyday life to elaborate legends of creation. Small children might hear the fable of how the rabbit got its long ears. An older audience would learn about their origins or the nature of the world. Each story had a purpose. During these intimate evenings, the children would come to understand and value bravery, respect the rights of others, and develop positive relations with everything in the universe.

One of my favorite memories as a child was sitting at the feet of my grandmother, listening to her recite the myths and legends that had been handed down by my ancestors. Legends stir the imagination. They allow children to do the impossible. Native Americans know this.

GAMES

All of these games were played by the Plains Indians BEFORE 1492!

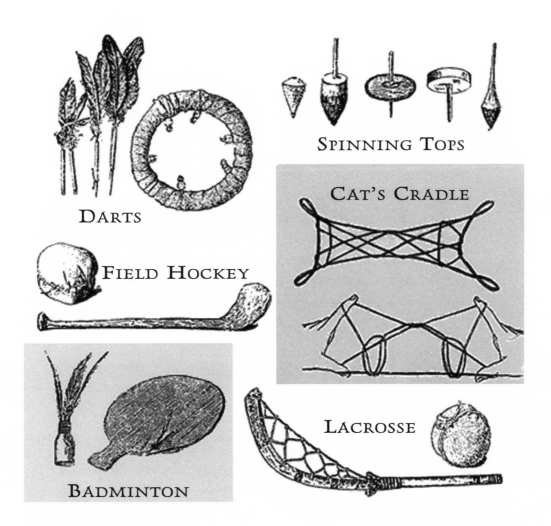

DARTS

SPINNING TOPS

FIELD HOCKEY

CAT'S CRADLE

BADMINTON

LACROSSE

THE LEGEND OF THE DREAM

Long ago when the word was young, an old Lakota spiritual leader was on a high mountain and had a vision. In his vision, Iktomi, the great trickster and teacher of wisdom, appeared in the form of a spider. Iktomi spoke to him in a sacred language. As he spoke, Iktomi the spider picked up the elder's willow hoop which had feathers, horsehair, beads and offerings on it, and began to spin a web.

He spoke to the elder about the cycles of life; how we begin our lives as infants, move on through childhood and on to adulthood. Finally we go to old age where we must be taken care of as infants, completing the cycle. "But," Iktomi said as he continued to spin his web, "in each time of life there are many forces; some good and some bad. If you listen to the good forces, they will steer you in the right direction. But, if you listen to the bad forces, they'll steer you in the wrong direction and may hurt you. So these forces can help, or can interfere with the harmony of Nature." While the spider spoke, he continued to weave his web.

*The Old Ones tell that
dreams hold great power
and drift about at night
before coming to the sleeping ones.
To keep the dreamers safe
the Old Ones created a special web,
the Dream Catcher,
to hang above their sleeping places.
When dreams traveled the web paths
the bad dreams lost their way and were entangled,
disappearing with the first rays of daybreak.
The good dreams, knowing the way,
passed through the center
and were guided gently
to the sleeping ones.*

CATCHER

When Iktomi finished speaking, he gave the elder the web and said, "The web is a perfect circle with a hole in the center. Use the web to help your people reach their goals, making good use of their ideas, dreams and visions. If you believe in the Great Spirit, the web will catch your good ideas and the bad ones will go through the hole." The elder passed on his vision to the people and now many Indian people hang a dream catcher above their bed to sift their dreams and visions. The good is captured in the web of life and carried with the people, but the evil in their dreams drops through the hole in the center of the web and are no longer a part of their lives. It's said that the dream catcher holds the destiny of the future.

DREAM CATCHER

Make your own dream catcher and hang it over your bed.

YOU WILL NEED:

craft glue

one 6 inch metal ring

pony beads

at least 8 yards of leather or suede lacing

2 yards of cotton cord

scissors

ruler

2 clothespins

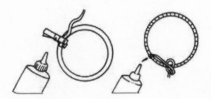

TO WRAP THE RING:

Spread glue on the first inch of your lacing. Fasten it on the ring with a clothespin. Carfefully wrap the lacing around the metal ring, making sure to keep the lacing flat. When you reach the place you started, put glue on the last inch of the lacing and hold both ends in place with the clothespin. Wait until the glue dries completely before going to the next step.

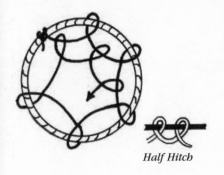

Half Hitch

TO TIE THE WEB:

Roll cotton cord loosely into a ball. Knot one end of cotton cord around the metal ring and seal the knot with glue. Tie approximately six half-hitches every three inches around the ring. (See illustration) Hold your completed knot tightly between your fingers as you begin the next half-hitch. Add another half-hitch next to the knot where you began. Now begin tying half hitches in the middle of the cord you already added. Continue until you complete a total of three more circles of half-hitches. Double knot the cord in the center of the web and seal the knot with glue. Cut off excess cord.

TO ADD THE HANGER:

Knot ends together of one 10-inch piece of leather lacing. Insert one end of loop through metal ring at the top. Draw knot through loop and pull tight.

TO ADD THE DANGLES:

Cut two 10-inch pieces of leather lacing and three 12-inch pieces. Knot one end of each piece. Thread pony beads onto each lace and knot the other end. Slide the same number of the beads up to each knot. Fold lacing in half and attach each piece the same way as the hanger.

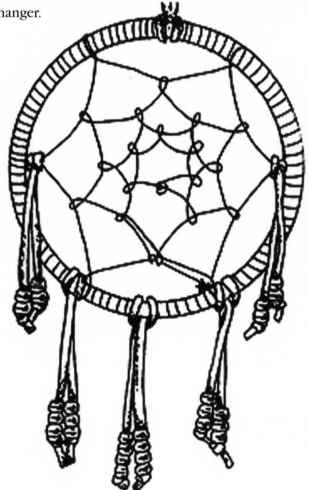

The end of childhood was signaled by adolescence. This was a major event for children and their community.

For a girl, it was a sign she had reached womanhood and could bear children. Spirit, or Towan, possessed her. Towan made her Wakan, or powerful. A Sioux father brought honor to himself and his family by hosting a ball throwing ceremony for his daughter, when she reached adolescence. Gifts would be collected, invitations extended to the entire community, and a great feast would be planned. At the end of the celebration, the girl would repeatedly throw a red ball into the crowd of guests. Each catch was rewarded with a rich gift from the girl's father. The feast followed the excitement.

All tribes celebrated a girl's rite of passage. The Apache staged elaborate ceremonies that lasted for days. The Cheyenne publicly announced the passage to adolescence from their tipi doors, and marked the occasion by giving away horses. Rituals, private or public, marked the celebration of a girl's adolescence in all Indian cultures.

Adolescent boys of the Great Plains idolized the tribe's war societies and there esteemed members. They memorized each society's rules and accomplishments, copied their regalia, and dreamed of the day they could join their favorite group.

In many tribes, boys could associate with societies established especially for youth. Blackfoot teenagers, for example, could join the Pigeon Society. This group was made up of boys who had not yet gone on a vision quest, but who wished to prepare for the duties of a warrior. Part of their training involved playing risky games and pranks. The elders tolerated these antics because they were believed to prepare the young boys for the hardships of war.

Among the Arapaho, boys entered one of two youth societies, the Blackbirds or the Wild Rosebushes. In these youth groups, boys learned some of the important skills that were required to join the real war societies. The Arapaho warrior societies were an organized progressive system. To graduate through the Arapaho ranks, men had to purchase the rights to the next level. The process would begin when a group of boys about the age of twelve felt they were ready to join the Kick Boxers. This was the lowest ranking Arapaho male war society. A boy's parents would pool their resources and collect goods and gifts. They would use these gifts to purchase their son's membership into the Kick Boxers from a current member. To close the deal, parents would often host a lavish feast. The younger boy did not join the Kick Boxers. Instead, he took a member's place. The older member then took these fees and used them to buy his way into the next highest level in the war society, the Stars. And so it continued up the ranks. The most senior members in the highest-ranking level sold out, retired from the system, and divided their large pile of wealth. Every few years this process repeated, as yet another group of adolescent boys came of age.

Adolescence
VISION QUESTS

Native Americans viewed success in life as a spiritual gift. In seeking this success, countless Indian youths undertook solitary journeys of discovery. They wished to experience a powerful, life-shaping dream. Through this dream, it was believed that an individual learned what special talents or abilities he or she possessed. These skills helped define the person's path in life. Adolescent boys and girls would begin these physically and emotionally demanding ordeals known as "vision quests."

Although details of the ordeal vary from tribe to tribe, most vision quests lasted between four and six days. Sioux youth spent the entire period in an earthen pit, naked except for a buffalo robe. Crow youth often slept inside a symbolic stone pit facing east, so the blessings of the morning sun would enter directly upon them. The seeker did not eat or drink during the quest. The most determined vision seekers often gouged bits of flesh from their arms or legs to make the spirits of nature take pity on them. Offerings of tobacco and other sacred items were also made.

The vision or dream might appear while the seeker was awake. It might come after exhaustion and hunger had caused a loss of consciousness. The dream most often contained animals or birds. The type of creature that appeared in the vision indicated which gift or power was being given to the youth. No animal outranked another. All animals were believed to have special powers or "medicine." To dream of a buffalo or bear brought no more status than dreaming about a turtle or a butterfly. If an adolescent received a dream during a vision quest, he or she would return home to the campsite and describe it to a shaman. The shaman would analyze the meaning behind the dream, and the youth's destiny was determined.

Although vision quests began in adolescence, they were practiced into adulthood. Many Plains people had numerous visions during their lifetimes. Others lived their entire lives without experiencing a single dream. Some tribes believed that good luck would come to those who kept trying. This good luck was a reward for their effort.

THE WAY OF THE WARRIOR

A new Plains Indian father held his baby son up to the heavens and prayed: "Oh Sun, make this boy strong and brave. May he die in battle rather than from old age or sickness." By the time the boy reached adolescence, he knew the trail to manhood was on the warpath. This was the way of the warrior, one who must always prove himself strong, brave, and courageous as a fighter or die trying.

The men of the Great Plains people were obsessed with planning, making and celebrating warfare. They could never possess enough horses. They wanted control of the best hunting grounds. And they fought to expand the boundaries of their homelands. These reasons were the cause of constant intertribal warfare during the Golden Era of the Horse on the Great Plains.

Warfare was closely connected to spirituality. Success at war depended upon every member of the tribe paying careful attention to the sacred ways at every step. The traditions were the same for hunting and planting crops. There were days of preparation before the raid. Then came the raiding journey to the enemy village. When the warriors returned there was a period of purification afterward. Warriors, women, boys and shamans all had specific roles to play. Plains Indians considered making war a necessary and honorable pursuit. However, they made a distinction between the "red road of war" and the "white road of peace." To a Plains Indian, the taking of any life, even that of an animal, was a solemn act that disrupted the balance and harmony of the universe. Only careful attention to rituals could protect men from the consequences of violent deeds. Because of this belief, warriors not only risked attack from their living enemies, but also from the spirits of the dead.

Cheyenne sundancers

A young man waited impatiently for the day he could take up arms and display the regalia of war. The clothing and gear of war was not only beautiful, but also full of enormous spiritual power. The wardrobe of a fighting man advertised his status and reputation within his community. Warriors donned elaborate war shirts. The fringed buckskin shirts were decorated with dyed porcupine quills and intricate beadwork, which gave its wearer powerful medicine for ceremonial occasions and for war. The deerskins used to make these shirts were cut as little as possible to show respect for the animal and to retain its power for the wearer. The fringes represented a connection to the Great Spirit, the creator of life. Locks of human hair, taken from enemies in battle, were often attached across the breast, celebrating the wearer's victories in war.

Special headdresses announced the presence of a war leader or other highly respected individual. Tribal warriors across the continent wore them in rituals before, during and after battle. The headdresses inspired bravery, displayed past war honors and called upon supernatural powers to succeed against one's enemies. The swept-back feathered headgear of the Lakota Sioux grew in popularity and eventually replaced the buffalo-horned war bonnet of earlier times. By the 19th century, the feathered headdress became the most recognizable piece of Native American regalia and the symbol of the warrior.

The headdress was typically made from golden eagle feathers. It was used to evoke the power of this magnificent bird of prey. It was intentionally designed to move in the breeze, imitating the powerful bird in flight. An individual warrior of his tribe contributed each of the feathers in a great chief's headdress, representing each warrior's acts of bravery. The chief went into battle wearing a symbol of communal spirit and the collective valor of his people.

Plains warriors also carried personal war bundles. They were assembled with the assistance of a shaman, who stipulated their contents and the special ceremonies governing their use. A typical bundle might contain an otterskin collar, deerskin leggings, a specially wrapped body of a hawk, an ear of corn, and paints in red, yellow and white. The most important color was red, the color of war. Some articles in the bundle were worn during battle to invoke spirit powers. Other items were used ritually before or after a battle.

Scabby Bull, Araphao

Indian warriors also carried a protective talisman. No Indian warrior would enter into battle without his personal token. It was often shield-shaped and assured the wearers that their guardian spirit was present, bringing the supernatural power needed for victory. The talisman gave the warrior added courage and he believed it would give strength to his arm and deflect enemy arrows. Amulets worn in the hair and around the neck warned enemies that they were facing not only human opponents, but spiritual ones as well.

A Plains warrior also carried a great shield into battle. The shield was decorated with symbols he saw in dreams or visions. Warriors believed that the symbols offered as much protection in battle as the thick buffalo hide they were painted upon. The shield was around 20–22 inches in diameter, and decorated with turtle shells, representing turtle medicine of good health and buffalo hooves representing the great animal they considered to be the center of the universe. Shields also displayed human scalp locks of fallen enemies and eagle feathers from the mightiest of the birds of prey.

The shield could deflect arrows, but not bullets. Still, they were prized for their supernatural protection during battle. The large shields used before the acquisition of the horse proved to be too bulky on horseback. They were replaced by smaller discs that were carried in front during an attack and slung across their back during retreat.

The loss of a shield was a major loss to a warrior because of its great power. When a warrior died, his shield was often buried with him, to protect him on his journey to the spirit world.

Then there were the weapons of war. A few tribes had a special craftsman who created weapons and earned the respect of his peers, but most warriors took great pride in creating their own weapons of war. Only a few chosen warriors were allowed to use spears and lances in battle, usually a token of their high status. Spears were hard to handle on horseback, but were efficient at taking down enemies during a charge. They were often adorned with feathers and scalps, proclaiming the acts of bravery and war skills of its bearer.

For a warrior on horseback, the bow and arrow was the weapon of choice. Bowstrings were made from buffalo sinew. The sinew was first softened by chewing and then twisted for strength. Bows were highly decorated with brain-tanned deerskin, fox tails, elaborate beadwork, and eagle feathers.

MOUNTED WARRIOR SHIELD

MATERIALS NEEDED:

wire coat hanger

large brown paper grocery bag

tempera paint

paintbrushes

crayons

yarn or twine

scissors

Decorative items that could include:
seashells, feathers, beads, bells, driftwood.

INSTRUCTIONS:

1. Bend the wire coat hanger to form a circle.

2. Cut the paper bag open on one side. Lay it flat and trace a circle one inch wider than the coat hanger's circle.

3. Cut out the paper circle and crinkle it until it resembles leather.

4. Sketch the shield's symbols with a crayon. Paint the symbols with earth-colored tempera paints.

5. Stretch the finished shield cover across the coat hanger. Wrap the edges of the paper around the wire circle.

6. Carefully punch holes along the edge of the shield. Thread yarn or twine through the holes to attach decorative items.

Project

Plains Indians often dismounted when they reached their target, but they still needed weapons that were easily carried on horseback and deployed from the mount if the need arose. As a result, bows became smaller, more than half the size of the original longbow. Some tribes discovered that they could craft compact sturdy bows from the horns of elk or bighorn sheep. Although these smaller bows were less powerful, warriors used them at closer range and fired more arrows. Some tribes made their arrows more deadly by coating the tips with poison.

Every warrior learned to make arrows from an early age. He picked a strip of wood about three feet long and less than one inch thick. He scraped off the bark and straightened the shaft by shaping it over hot coals. Next, he tapered and notched the butt of the arrow for the bowstring. Feathers split down their spine were lashed to the shaft just in front of the notch. Feathers were added to provide stability in flight. The arrowhead was usually chipped from flint, quartz, or obsidian. The arrowhead was wedged into a slot at the front of the shaft and bound tightly with sinew. Arrows, like bows, were decorated with distinctive markings to identify the owner. Because they put so much effort into crafting these arrows, warriors went to great lengths to recover them.

Colonists were impressed by both the speed and strength of Indian bowman, who could unleash several arrows in the time it took Europeans to load and fire a single shot from a musket.

Warrior

Nearly every warrior carried a war club. These handy weapons were fashioned in various ways. Sometimes a warrior dug up a young sapling when it was only a few inches tall. This was the handle. The root ball formed the "business end" of the club. Sometimes the roots were trimmed down and sharpened into spikes. A warrior might also add a heavy round stone or chiseled blade to the wooden shaft. A direct blow from a stone club could bring death to an enemy.

It was only after Europeans made metal-bladed hatchets widely available that the Indians began producing a weapon called the tomahawk. At first, Indians chiseled down obsidian to form hatchet blades and attached them with rawhide to a wooden shaft. After the introduction of forged metal, Indians replaced the stone blade with one made of iron. Warriors became experts at throwing their tomahawks.

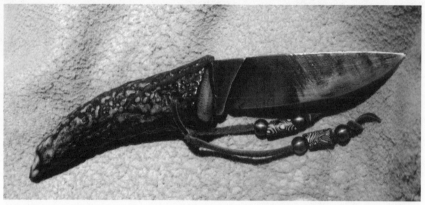

Knives were also part of a warrior's arsenal. Early knives were fashioned from stone blades. Handles were made from elk or deer horn. The blade was secured with rawhide or sinew. After the introduction of forged metal by Europeans, the fragile stone blade was replaced by iron. Knives were stored in elaborately decorated leather sheaths, worn proudly on a warrior's belt. Sometimes a smaller knife was concealed in a warrior's moccasin or leggings.

Eventually the Buffalo People acquired a weapon that would dramatically change the tactical aspects of war. At first the Plains Indians dreaded the noise, fire and smoke of the musket. Then they quickly learned to understand its mysteries and became devoted to it. The Sioux called the gun "medicine iron." In a short time, braves were trading horses for guns one for one. Warriors looked for guns that were lightweight and easy to carry into battle. Sometimes Plains Indians filed down the barrel to make it shorter and easier to handle. These weapons were called Northwest Trade guns. They first reached the Indians through the hands of immigrant fur traders. Traders offered the guns in exchange for buffalo hides or sleek and valuable fox pelts. The shooting accuracy of these "trade guns" were very limited. If a warrior shortened the barrel, this also decreased the firing range of the gun.

A greater inconvenience for the warrior was the time and trouble it took to reload a muzzle-loading rifle. Warriors developed faster ways to reload. One trick was to carry spare lead balls in their mouth while riding and spit them down the barrel onto the powder charge. This allowed the warrior to skip the ramrod and get off 4–5 rounds in the space of a minute or so. As with their other weapons, Plains Indians gave European firearms spiritual powers. They decorated the gunstock with brass tacks in elaborate sacred designs.

The warrior ethic was so deeply imbedded in the hearts and minds of the Plains Indians, that they became more interested in the competitive challenge of warfare than the riches they could acquire or any harm done to their enemies. Warriors were honored for killing or scalping an enemy, for capturing enemy weapons and successful horse raids. But the ultimate act of bravery was to touch one's enemy with a stick or staff without drawing blood. This deed was known as "counting coup" (Pronounced coo, from the French word for "blow"). The daring required for counting coup brought a Plains Indian warrior much more honor than simply shooting the enemy at a distance with a bow or gun.

A warrior attempted to touch the enemy with a "coup stick." The coup stick could be anywhere from one to ten feet in length. Most coup sticks were wrapped with animal skin or fur. They were decorated with beadwork, turtle shells, animal skulls, teeth and claws, deer or buffalo hooves as well as eagle feathers. All these were designed to evoke the powerful medicine of these animals. The Plains warriors believed that a coup stick was so powerful and supernaturally charged they were convinced that a single touch of this weapon would absorb the soul of their enemy.

Warrior

This would put them in control of their enemy's spirit. If touched by an enemy's coup stick, a warrior would lose all status and would be forced to leave his tribe. The counting of coup was so important to the Sioux, Crow, Arapaho and other tribes that they sometimes went to battle armed only with a coup stick.

In time, the term "coup" was also used to describe other feats of bravery, including scalping the enemy, stealing a war horse or buffalo runner tethered outside an enemy's tipi, stealing a bow or gun during hand-to-hand combat, touching an enemy's tipi or leaping over a fallen opponent on horseback. These acts were each rewarded with a single eagle feather, which the brave would wear to display his accomplishments.

Warrior

With all these weapons at his disposal, no weapon was more valuable to a Plains Indian warrior than a good horse. Warriors brought along two mounts into battle whenever possible. One sturdy animal was for the trail. The other was a swift and courageous war-horse for the battle. The bond of brotherhood between the Indian and his horse was a mental, physical and spiritual connection. It was an unspoken language of trust, respect and loyalty. Training together, the warrior and his horse became as one, moving in unison with ease and elegance. A Plains Indian was more comfortable astride his horse than on solid ground. A mounted warrior could pick up an object from the ground at a full gallop. He could also ride backward while shooting arrows at his enemies. One of the most amazing feats was a warrior hooking one leg across the horse and riding along the horse's flank to avoid enemy fire.

Most Plains warriors did not use traditional saddle with stirrups. Instead, they rode upon a blanket or buffalo hide pad and controlled the horse with a single rein looped across the horse's lower jaw. Since the warrior needed both hands to fire a bow or gun during battle, the horse also was trained to obey voice commands and respond to cues from the rider's legs. On the battlefield, a warrior might suddenly dismount, be pulled off by an enemy, or both horse and rider could go down. A warhorse was trained to remain calm and close by, ready for his rider to remount.

Many times, victory went to the enemy and a warrior would make a daring attempt to flee his foe on horseback. Swinging from one flank to another, or even under the galloping horse's powerful neck, the escaping warrior presented a difficult target.

Most riderless horses were rounded up and claimed by the victors. The horses that escaped would later return to the scene of the battle to search for their fallen rider. A war-horse would even lie down in order to allow his wounded rider to mount more easily. Sometimes a faithful war-horse would stand over his fallen rider's body for days, until forced by hunger and thirst to leave his beloved partner. Warriors would often attempt to return to the battlefield to find their fallen mounts and mercifully put them to rest. They would gather hoofs and hair from the mane and tail of the fallen horse. These were made into horse honoring dance sticks, or included as part of future horse regalia. This was a reminder of their fallen brother's bravery and dedication.

Native American Coup Stick

Materials Needed:

a stick (measuring approximately ¹/₂" diameter by 2' long)

yarn

Synthetic fur scraps

2 bells

12 inch piece of suede lacing

pony beads

feathers

clear-drying glue

scissors

Construct Your Coup Stick

Cut a small piece of fur and cover the back side with glue. Then wrap it around the end of the stick. Spread a thin layer of glue on the stick just below the fur. Wrap colored yarn tightly around the stick. Add more glue as you continue to wrap the yarn for about 5", changing colors if desired.

Tie the suede lacing just below where the yarn wrap ends. Slide the bells onto the lacing and tie in a knot. String several pony beads onto each end of the lacing. Tie a knot on each end to secure the beads. Attach feathers to the stick by sliding the quill end of the feather through the center of the pony beads. Add a drop of glue to each bead to secure the feather.

There was no set pattern for making a coup stick. The above is merely a suggestion. Designs and decorations varied greatly and were highly individual. Some coup sticks were 6 feet in length, others only 24 inches long. Deerskin fringe might be found on one warrior's stick, while another chose to cover his weapon with sheered beaver fur. Elaborately beaded and painted coup sticks were as common as those with much simpler designs. Be creative and use your own personal touches.

Traditional Warrior's Breastplate

Items Needed

80 white plastic drinking straws

300 pony beads

1 skein of brown yarn (4 ounces)

Construct Breastplate

1. String beads and straws in this order, making sure to leave a 3-inch tail of yarn on each end: 3 inches of yarn + one pony bead + one drinking straw + two pony beads + one drinking straw + one pony bead + three inches of yarn

2. Tie a knot the next to the bead in each end of the yarn.

3. Repeat steps 1 and 2 until you have completed 40 pieces. (More if you are taller, less if you are shorter.)

4. Lay all the pieces on a flat surface. Starting at the top of one side, assemble the breastplate by first wrapping yarn two times between the end bead and the straw. Continue until all pieces are attached.

5. When you have completed one side, continue by stringing 20 pony beads on the yarn to hand in a half-circle below the breastplate. Secure the yarn between the two center beads and string another 20 pony beads. Secure the yarn between the end bead and the straw on the opposite side.

6. Repeat step 5, working up the other side of the breastplate.

7. Now create the neckpiece. When you have completely fastened all pieces, string approximately 30 pony beads and attach the yarn at the top of the other side of the breastplate.

Warrior

PAINT OF WAR

Hand-to-hand combat was recorded and symbolized by the warrior's red handprint.

A successful horse raid was displayed with angular horse hoof symbols in yellow paint.

Warriors revered their courageous war horses. Before entering into battle, a warrior painted his brave steed with ritual symbols. Using his mount as a billboard, a warrior tried to intimidate his enemy with a colorful display of his heroic accomplishments. He also painted markings of spiritual powers that the horse and rider possessed. Because of the close bond between warrior and horse, a Plains Indian painted his horse in the same pattern as he did his own body.

A Plains Indian used things abundant in nature to make war paint. Paints were stored in the form of dried powder and each color stored in its own deerskin pouch, which made them easier to transport. The colors available were very limited. Brown paint came from the rich brown earth. Black was derived from charcoal and ashes. Algae was dried for the color green. Red was sometimes derived from red clay but more often from the root of a plant named bloodroot. True to its name, the color came from the root and not the plant itself. The root was dried and ground to produce a rich red color. White came from chalk found in the area. Blue came from birds that enjoyed eating wild blueberries, most often, wild ducks and geese. Yellow most often came from buffalo gallstones.

Paint pot made from stone.

In order to apply the paint, the Indian mixed the dry powder with buffalo fat to make a grease paint in a paint pot. A paint pot was made from a large stone hollowed out by using a smaller stone. Unbreakable and easy to carry, they were often passed from generation to generation. Powder was mixed with buffalo fat and stirred with a stick. It was often applied to the horse using a sponge-like material found in the hipbone of the buffalo.

Animal symbols were painted to evoke the powerful medicine of these creatures and to provide the horse with additional strength for battle.

Horses also wore eagle feathers tied into the mane and tail, symbolizing courage and swiftness.

The turtle symbol was for protection, ensuring good health and long life.

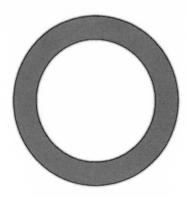

The symbol of a deer antler was used to give the horse the speed and stamina to sprint.

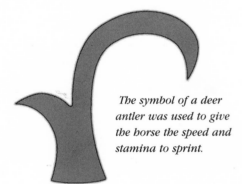

A round circle of red paint was often applied around one eye of a war horse. This was believed to give the animal exceptional eyesight and the ability to stare into the souls of the enemy.

Horses also had painted symbols of the injuries they had received and survived from previous battles. Bleeding round spots or slashes of red paint indicated the wounds.

Round white hailstones painted on a horse's shoulders and rump were intended to bring down the force of a terrible storm upon the enemy.

A mounted warrior would often run down an enemy on foot. To symbolize this accomplishment, a figure of a flattened man would be painted on the horse's chest.

A butterfly symbol was used to help the horse avoid enemy arrows and bullets.

Spiritual symbols were also painted. Yellow lightning bolts down the horse's legs called upon the spiritual aid and guidance of the Thunderbird.

Bear claw gashes painted in red symbolized the ferocity of a bear on the battlefield.

Warriors painted red or black horizontal lines on their horse's rump and nose. The lines represented previous acts of bravery.

CHIEFS AND LEADERSHIP

Red Cloud

Generosity, honor, loyalty, and bravery were ideals that shaped and defined the people of the Plains. This was reflected in their choice of leaders. A great chief had much knowledge of his people and their traditions.

Luther Standing Bear, a Lakota Sioux, explained about chiefs, "In their minds were stored the history and lore of the tribe, the events of migration and travel, the tales and prophecies of wise men, battles and victories, and secrets the brotherhood of animals shared with the medicine men.

Above all a chief must be a giver and not a receiver – a man of self-denial."

The Great Plains Indian chiefs devoted all their physical, emotional, and spiritual strength to the welfare of the community. Even though they worked very hard for the good of the people, they had to be ready to give up command at any time. Peacetime leaders were chosen for their wisdom and judgment. War chiefs were selected for their courage and prowess in battle.

The majority of the Plains tribes had a number of chiefs. For example, the Cheyenne had forty-four. There were four principal chiefs and four lesser chiefs from each of the tribe's ten bands. They held regular council, at which they made the major decisions about the welfare of the tribe. They might decide when to hold a group buffalo hunt or whether the tribe should go to war.

Warrior

A chief also had to resolve the smaller day-to-day problems that arose in his band. His primary duty was to look out for the welfare of widows and children, whose husbands and fathers had been killed in battle or while hunting. A chief's next obligation was to settle quarrels between members of the tribe. A chief never took part in arguments himself, nor did he use his position to enrich himself or his family.

Plenty Coups

A WAR QUEST

Although no one knows when scalping began in North America, the custom was well established by the time the first white man reached the continent. Scalp taking typically involved removing a patch of skin and hair approximately six inches in diameter from the crown of the skull.

For some tribes, a preserved enemy scalp was not only a reward for fighting, but also an important reason for doing battle in the first place. Native Americans believed that the patch of skin on the top of the head and the hair that grew represented the warrior's living spirit. To symbolize this, a warrior might wear his hair in a single lock, or scalp lock. He usually braided and decorated this section of hair with feathers and other ornaments that marked his achievements and honors. For a warrior to touch the scalp lock of another was an insult. Even though a man might survive a scalping, he became an outcast in the eyes of his peers. Losing all honor and status was considered a fate worse than death.

Certain tribes on the Great Plains, such as the Sioux, initiated scalp raids against the enemy in order to replace the lost spiritual essence of a tribal member who had recently been killed. Bringing home the enemy scalp was intended to lessen the grief of family survivors. This grief was so intense, that widows thrashed about and often gashed themselves with knives. Some women used the hair of the scalp to dry their tears while they were in mourning.

For every warrior, scalps collected from the enemy were the ultimate quest. When attained, they were proudly displayed on all war regalia and weaponry. Some were attached to lances, shields, and coup sticks. Others were sewn across the breast and shoulders of a fighting man's war shirt. It celebrated victories on the battlefield and further enhanced the supernatural powers of this prestigious article of clothing. To boast accomplishments as an invincible team, it was common for a single preserved scalp lock to be fastened to the bridle of a warrior's equine comrade.

Although Europeans did not introduce scalping, they supplied momentum for the practice, when they put a price on the scalps of their enemies. It changed what had formerly been a ritual act into a commercial business. Scalping became an industry. The Dutch first started it, and later the French and the English followed suit. The market for enemy scalps boomed. Within a century, colonists were offering a bounty equal to $134.00 for an adult male scalp taken from a hostile party.

Hunting on

HUNTING TATANKA

Hunting the buffalo with horses made the traditional longbow obsolete. It was too large to be practical on horseback. A much shorter bow now served the purpose because the horse allowed the hunters to get much closer to the buffalo and escape quickly.

Each hunter filled his quiver with 12-24 arrows. Each arrow bore that hunter's personal mark. This made it very easy for each hunter to identify his kill. The runner was fitted with a buffalo hide saddle-like pad, secured by a girth strap made from a wide band of soft rawhide. The hunter left the girth loose so that he could put his knees under the girth to brace himself during the chase. The bridle was made of a thin rawhide thong, looped over the horse's lower jaw. During the chase, the reins were tucked into his belt. This left both hands free to shoot the bow. At the climax of the hunt, only the rider's knees guided the horse, shifting his weight to indicate the direction he wanted to ride.

Hunters started the buffalo hunt downwind from the herd, getting as close as possible without being detected. The skilled hunter knew every muscle, bone, and sinew of this great beast. When he was within 25 feet, he would shoot an arrow. The hunter aimed for a vulnerable spot, like the area behind the last rib. If it struck here, the arrow only traveled a short distance before doing great internal damage. With luck, the arrow might also pierce a major organ so the animal would drop quickly. Sometimes, a buffalo would run 1-2 miles before collapsing. It often required 2-3 arrows to bring an adult buffalo down.

Horseback

During the hunt there were many dangers for the hunter and his horse. An injured buffalo might turn and charge, attempting to gore the horse with its horns. To avoid this kind of injury, hunters trained their mounts to veer away sharply the instant they heard the sharp twang of the bowstring.

The hunt and chase lasted for approximately 30 minutes. The hunters would then dismount and lead their horses back through the field of dead and dying buffalo. They finished off any wounded buffalo, searched for their arrows, and marked their kills.

The young boys of the tribe followed the hunters on their own ponies. They practiced their hunting skills on any calves that may have been left behind. This was their chance to prepare for the day they would be the hunters.

A hunter was only as good as his runner. A skilled hunter on a well-trained runner could bring down as many as 4–5 buffalo in a single chase. A novice hunter could bring down perhaps 2 animals during a chase. This provided enough meat to feed an extended family of a dozen members for two weeks.

Since the horse allowed the Indians to move with ease, hunters were able to stay in touch with the great herds, hunting as needed for months on end. Over the course of a year, 20 hunters could bring down as many as 1,000 buffalo. The abundance of food helped the Plains Indians become prosperous and their populations grew.

HUNTING WILD HORSES

There were many herds of wild horses roaming the Great Plains. Many of these horses who "ran wild" were a result of getting loose during the skirmishes between the Indians and the Spanish colonists. Others, that were lame or needed resting, were probably turned loose, their owners intending to round them up later. Some domestic horses put out to graze on the range simply wandered off. Gradually these horses joined together to form feral herds, which flourished on the wide-open spaces of the Great Plains. When nomadic tribes spotted these roaming herds of wild horses, all tribal members shared great excitement. A carefully planned horse roundup was always a call for celebration.

Every man was to participate, and all worked together. Some gathered very long willow sticks, some fifteen feet in length, from a nearby creek. Others would gather up their strongest buffalo hide ropes. The long braided ropes were made into nooses. They were attached to the willow sticks with strips of soft buckskin.

Men saddled up their swift runners and were dressed as if they were going buffalo hunting. Their horses were specifically trained for the hunt. It made no difference to the horses whether they were to hunt Tatanka or other horses. They were eager for the chase.

The roundup party would divide into four groups. Three groups would ride two or three miles out onto the prairie, positioning themselves to the north, south, and west of the grazing herd. The party carrying the willow sticks with nooses remained to the east side of the wild herd, waiting patiently for the right moment.

The party that had gone over to the west side would make the first move, taking off in unison at a full gallop. As soon as the wild horses saw them, they bolted. If the herd ran to the north, the northern roundup party would head them off. If the frightened horse herd veered to the south, once again, the southern group would turn them. The wild animals would frantically race together in hopes of finding escape. This game of "chase and turn" continued until the herd was near the brink of exhaustion. Eventually, they were steered to the east, where the party with sticks and nooses was just waiting.

The wild horses had already run quite a distance and found it difficult to keep up the pace of the pursuit. The eastern group was all
ready for them; their runners were fresh and anxious to go. The men
would whip up their horses and give chase.

A rider would select a target and guide his runner with just his legs
directly behind the wild horse. Firmly grasping his own horse's
mane with one hand, he would raise his stick with his free arm and
lower the noose over the wild horse's head. Next, the rider would
urge his own horse faster until he was almost alongside the wild
animal. The loop was wide open and slid down his target's neck. He
would give the stick a quick jerk. This broke the buckskin strings
that tied the rawhide rope to the stick, and the stick was discarded.
By this time, the wild horse was beginning to falter. The end of the
rope was thrown over the head of his runner, well down on the
neck. At the same time, he guided his horse away from the captured
animal. When the loop tightened, the wild horse began to choke.
Suddenly, it would come to a complete stop. Breathing heavily, it
would stagger a bit then fall to the ground.

Hunting on

Time was of the essence. The rider would quickly dismount and race over to the downed horse. With great skill and ease, he formed a halter of the long rope and firmly secured it around his captive's nose. Immediately, he ran to his runner, tied up his tail, and backed him over the head of the captured animal. The free end of the halter rope was first tied to the tail of his own horse, then brought around the shoulders, and back to the tail again. This would make the pull entirely on the shoulders and chest of his runner.

When the wild horse regained its breath and jumped to its feet, it discovered a very bewildering situation. Its nose was buried in the tail of another horse. If it tried to move away, it was pulling against its own nose. The captured horse had no choice but to follow. Behind the strong buffalo runner, the confused, exhausted, animal was quickly led back to camp.

As the roundup party returned, cheers came from all the tribal members. That evening, a celebration feast would take place to honor the hunters, their splendid runners, and the acquisition of the valuable new horses.

Horseback

As told by...

Crowfoot

Blackfoot

CROWFOOT
BLACKFOOT WARRIOR AND ORATOR

"What is life? It is the flash of a firefly in the night. It is the breath of a buffalo in the wintertime. It is the little shadow which runs across the grass and loses itself in the sunset."

FLYING HAWK
SOUTH DAKOTA OGLALA SIOUX (1852–1931)

"The tipi is much better to live in; always clean, warm in winter, cool in summer, easy to move... If the Great Spirit wanted men to live in one place he would have made the world stand still."

A LAKOTA PRAYER

"O Wakan-Tanka (Great Spirit), You have taught us your will through Tatanka, the chief of the Four-leggeds. You O Tatanka are the fruit of our Mother Earth from which we live. Here on Earth we live together with You O Tatanka and we are grateful to You; for it is you who give us our food and makes the people happy."

FLAT-IRON
OGLALA SIOUX CHIEF

"From Wakan-Tanka, the Great Mystery, comes all power. It is from Wakan-Tanka that the holy man has wisdom and the power to heal and make holy charms. Man knows that all healing plants are given by Wakan-Tanka, therefore they are holy. So too is the buffalo holy, because it is the gift of Wakan-Tanka."

BLACK ELK
OGLALA SIOUX HOLY MAN
(1863–1950)

"You have noticed that everything as Indian does is in a circle, and that is because the Power of the World always works in circles, and everything tries to be round...

"The Sky is round, and I have heard that the earth is round like a ball, and so are all the stars. The wind, in its greatest power, whirls. Birds make their nest in circles, for theirs is the same religion as ours...

"Even the seasons form a great circle in their changing, and always come back again to where they were. The life of a man is a circle from childhood to childhood, and so it is in everything where power moves."

ANCIENT INDIAN PROVERB

Treat the earth well: it was not given to you by your parents, it was loaned to you by your children. We do not inherit the Earth from our Ancestors, we borrow it from our Children.

CHIEF SEATTLE

(1786–1866)

"How can you buy or sell the sky, the warmth of the land? The idea is strange to us. If we do not own the freshness of the air and the sparkle of the water, how can you buy them? Every part of this earth is sacred to my people. Every shining pine needle, every sandy shore, every mist in the dark woods, every clearing and humming insect is holy in the memory and experience of my people. The sap, which courses through the trees, carries the memories of the red man.

"The white man's dead forget the country of their birth when they go walk among the stars. Our dead never forget this beautiful earth, for it is the mother of the red man. We are part of the earth and it is part of us. The perfumed flowers are our sisters; the deer, the horse, the great eagle, these are our brothers. The rocky crests, the juices in the meadows, the body heat of the pony, and man - all belong to the same family. So, when the Great Chief in Washington sends word that he wishes to buy our land, he asks much of us.

"This shining water that moves in the streams and rivers is not just water but the blood of our ancestors. If we sell you land, you must remember that it is sacred, and you must teach your children that it is sacred and that each ghostly reflection in the clear water of the lakes tells us events and memories in the life of my people. The water's murmur is the voice of my father's father.

"The rivers are our brothers, they quench our thirst. The rivers carry our canoes, and feed our children. If we sell you our land, you must remember to teach your children that the rivers are our brothers, and yours, and you must henceforth give the rivers the kindness you would give any brother.

"We know that the white man does not understand our ways. One portion of land is the same to him as the next, for he is a stranger who comes in the night and takes from the land whatever he needs. The earth is not his brother, but his enemy, and when he has conquered it, he moves on. He leaves his fathers' graves behind and he does not care. His fathers' graves and his children's birthright are forgotten. He treats his mother, the earth, and his brother, the sky as things to be bought, plundered, sold like sheep or bright beads. His appetite will devour the earth and leave behind only desert.

"The air is precious to the red man, for all things share the same breath - the beast, the man, they all share the same breath. The white man does not seem to notice the air he breathes. Like a man dying for many days, he is numb to the stench. But if we sell you our land, you must remember that the air is precious to us, that the air shares its spirit with all life it supports. The wind that gave our grandfather his first breath also receives his last sigh. And if we sell you our land, you must keep it apart and sacred as a place where even the white man can go to taste the wind that is sweetened by the meadow's flowers.

"We will consider your offer to buy our land. If we decide to accept, I will make one condition: the white man must treat the beasts of this land as his brothers. What is man without the beasts? If the beasts were gone, men would die from a great loneliness of spirit. For whatever happens to the beasts, soon happens to man. All things are connected.

"Teach your children what we have taught our children—that the earth is our mother. Whatever befalls the earth befalls the sons of the earth. If men spit upon the ground, they spit upon themselves. Whatever befalls the earth befalls the sons of the earth. Man did not weave the web of life, he is merely a strand in it. Whatever he does to the web, he does to himself.

"Even the white man, whose God walks and talks with him as friend to friend, cannot be exempt from common destiny. We may be brothers after all. We shall see. One thing we know, which the white man may one day discover, our God is the same God. You may think now that you own Him as you wish to own our land, but you cannot. He is the God of man, and His compassion is equal for the red man and the white. This hearth is precious to Him and to harm the earth is to heap contempt on its Creator. The whites, too, shall pass; perhaps sooner than all other tribes. Contaminate your bed and you will one night suffocate in your own waste."

Buffalo

A PLAINS INDIAN LEGEND

In the First Days, a powerful being called Humpback owned all the buffalo. He kept them in his corral high in the mountains, where he lived with his young son. Humpback would not release a single buffalo for the people of the Earth. He would not share any meat with the creatures that lived near him.

Coyote decided that something must be done to release the buffalo. He called the people to a council. "Humpback will not share any buffalo," said Coyote. "Let us all go to his corral and make a plan to release them ourselves."

They camped in the mountains near Humpback's home. After dark they inspected the buffalo corral. The stone walls were much too high to climb. The only entrance was through the back door of Humpback's house. For four days they continued to watch Humpback and his son and wait.

Coyote gathered them together for another council. "Does anyone have a plan to release the buffalo?" Coyote asked.

"There is no way for us to release the buffalo," said one man. "Humpback is too powerful for us."

"I have a plan," said Coyote. "Have you not seen that Humpback's son has no pet?"

The people did not understand what this meant. But they knew Coyote was a great trickster, so they waited for him to explain. "I shall change myself into a killdeer," said Coyote. "In the morning, when Humpback's son comes for spring water, he will find a small bird with a broken wing. He will want the bird for a pet. When he takes me into the house, I can fly into the corral. The killdeer cries will stampede the buffalo, sending them charging through Humpback's house. Then the buffalo will be released upon the Earth."

The people agreed that this was a good plan. Humpback's son came to the spring the next morning. Along the path he found a killdeer with an injured wing. As Coyote predicted, the boy picked up the bird and carried it into the house.

WERE RELEASED

"Look here, Father," said the boy. "This is a very good bird."

"It is good for nothing!" shouted Humpback. "All the birds and animals and people are rascals and tricksters!"

"But it is a very good bird, Father," answered the boy.

"Take it back where you found it!" roared Humpback.

The frightened boy did what he was told. As soon as the killdeer was released, he flew back to the waiting people. "I have failed," he said. "But I will try again tomorrow. Perhaps a small animal will be better than a bird."

The next morning the boy found a small dog lapping water at the spring. He happily picked up the dog and hurried home. "Look here, Father. See what a nice pet I have!" he exclaimed.

"Foolish boy!" growled Humpback. "A dog is good for nothing. I will kill it with my club!"

But the boy held the dog tightly and ran away crying.

"Oh, very well," said Humpback. "You may keep it. But not in the house. Put it in the buffalo corral."

This was exactly what Coyote wanted. As soon as it was dark, he ran among the buffalo, barking as loud as he could. The frightened buffalo stampeded through Humpback's house, with Coyote nipping at their heels. Humpback woke at the sound of pounding hooves, but it was too late. The buffalo smashed down his front door and escaped.

After the last buffalo thundered off, Humpback's son looked for his dog. "Where is my dear pet?" he cried.

"That was no dog," said Humpback sadly. "That was surely Coyote the Trickster. He has set all our buffalo free."

And so it was that the buffalo were released and scattered over the Earth.

AMERICAN BUFFALO

The American buffalo once roamed the Great Plains in herds that numbered millions. This animal was the source of life for the Plains Indians. More than 20 million buffalo still thundered across western North America in 1850. As the Europeans expanded westward, the huge herds often forced railroad trains to stop as they crossed the tracks. The dust cloud raised by the migrating animals could be seen for miles and the ground would rumble.

During the next 30 years, European hunters slaughtered millions of the great beasts. The hunting was not even sporting. Tourists were allowed to shoot from trains. Often, only the hides and tongues were collected, leaving behind fields of rotting carcasses. The Indians were shocked and dismayed at the great insult to the Great Spirit. 1889 found only 551 bison alive in all of North America. Not only did the buffalo nearly become extinct, the loss of their main source of food almost wiped out the Plains Indians too.

An American zoologist named William Temple Hornaday (1854–1937) worked hard to protect and preserve the remaining bison. As a result of his efforts, more than 15,000 buffalo survive today on game preserves in the United States. An equal number of bison are found in the enormous Wood Buffalo National Park in Canada. There are also several thousand bison raised for meat on private ranches in both the U.S. And Canada.

Most of us call the large humped beast of the Great Plains a "buffalo." Scientists, however, consider this animal a "bison." Whatever name you use, Tatanka is the largest mammal surviving on the North American continent.

Tatanka is brownish-black on the head and shoulders. The hind part of the body is a lighter brownish-red. Long coarse hair covers the head, neck and hump. A mature buffalo also wears a beard on its throat and chin. Their appearance caused the immigrant Europeans to nickname the buffalo "Great Shaggies."

Buffalo have a pair of horns, similar to domestic cattle. Some mature bulls sport a pair of horns that spread nearly three feet. Full-grown by age eight, an adult male can measure 10–12 feet long from the tip of his nose to the end of his short, tufted tail. Standing six feet tall at the shoulder, a bull usually weighs between 1,600 and 2,000 pounds. Some exceptional bulls weigh as much as 3,000 pounds. Female buffalo are called cows. Cows are much smaller than bulls, often weighing less than 900 pounds.

Buffalo did not travel together in a dense, social herd of thousands. Instead, they dispersed and grazed quietly together in little families. These families consisted of two distinct groups – the nursery bands made up cows and their young, and the bull groups made up of mature bulls. The nursery bands contained anywhere from a few dozen to several hundred animals, including cows, calves, yearlings, and two-year-olds. A single, experienced matriarch led them all. The bull groups stayed together in clusters of a few to as many as thirty animals.

The buffalo in the bull and cow-calf bands came together by the thousands only in July and August for the rutting, or mating, season. During this time, bulls would ferociously compete to gain control of the cow bands. They engaged in head-butting contests that continued until one of the two competitors accepted defeat and retreated. Sometimes the duel ended in death. Peace returned with the coming of fall. The victorious bulls peacefully remained with the calves and cows for a time, and moved on when winter approached. In the spring a cow gave birth to a single calf.

No longer hunted, bison have been known to live as long as 30-40 years. Being herbivores, buffalo survived in huge numbers by grazing on the ocean of grass on the Great Plains. Some cattle ranchers have crossed American Buffalo with domestic cattle. The resulting hybrid (called Beefalo or Cattalo), feed on grass and don't need the addition of costly grain in their diet to fatten up for market.

Buffalo

How many buffalo roamed the Great Plains of North America in 1800? The accepted figure is more than 60 million animals. But how many is that really? Ed Park, author of "The World of the Bison," offers a visual representation:

"Imagine a long, single–file column of buffalo, head to tail, walking past you, one every two seconds. Take a counter and start counting them — one every two seconds, hour after hour, day after day — without pause. During the first minute 30 buffalo would file past; in the first hour 1,800 would go by. If you could stay awake for the first twenty-four hours, you would count 43,200 buffalo. The days would roll by and sometime during the twenty-fourth day the one-millionth buffalo would hurry past. Months would drag by, the seasons would change, and you would become tired of counting. Buffalo adding up to several millions would have passed before your eyes in seemingly endless file, with still more to come. At the end of the first year your counter would show a total of 15,768,000 buffalo. But the end would not be in sight! The second year would pass, then the third, and finally the fourth, with even an extra day added for a leap year. As the fourth year drew to a close, the last buffalo would hurry by, and you could look at your counter one last time! 63,115,200!"

THE BUFFALO NICKEL

The first bag of Buffalo Nickels were presented to President Taft and 33 Native American chiefs on March 14, 1913. They were gathered to take part in the groundbreaking ceremony for the National Memorial to the North American Indian at Fort Wadsworth, New York.

Artist and sculptor James Earle Fraser created the design for the new coin. Prior to this time, most Native Americans portrayed on United States coins were simply Caucasians wearing an Indian headdress. Fraser used several Plains Indian chiefs as models for the authentic portrait. No one can say for sure which individuals actually posed for Fraser. Historians believe that three different men posed for the portrait. The names history mentions include Chief John Big Tree, Chief Iron Tail, Chief Two Moons and Chief Two Guns White Calf.

On the reverse side of the coin is an American Bison. For his model Fraser chose Black Diamond, a famous resident of the New York City Zoo. By the late 1880's, the millions of buffalo that once roamed the Great Plains had been hunted to near extinction. For Fraser, the buffalo was a "perfect unity of theme" with the chief on the other side of the coin. Awareness of the buffalo's plight was an unexpected benefit of the Buffalo nickel. James Earle Fraser was born in Winona, Minnesota in 1876. He spent his boyhood in the Dakota Territory. Growing up on the Great Plains, Fraser saw the westward advance of "civilization." He also watched the gradual removal of the Native American people from their native land. Fraser used these childhood memories to create a lasting tribute to these Buffalo People. Fraser began his art studies in the studio of Richard Bock in Chicago and at the Art Institute of Chicago. He went to Paris in 1894, where he enrolled at the world-famous Ecole des Beaux Arts. Another Paris-trained American sculptor, Augustus Saint-Gaudens, noticed the talented young Fraser. Saint-Gaudens helped Fraser develop his talent as a sculptor.

In 1900 Fraser returned to the United States and opened a small studio in New York. Here he specialized in portrait busts of children. In 1913, he was commissioned to design the Buffalo/Indian Head nickel.

Fraser's most famous sculpture, The End of the Trail, was a work he began modeling early in his career. He recreated in several forms and sizes through 1929. It showed a stooped and dejected Native American brave on his exhausted and windblown horse. It was the icon for the defeat of the Native American in the now "American" West.

Fraser was inspired by a visit to the Chicago World's Fair of 1893. There, he saw other statues of cowboys and Indians. He sadly realized that the frontier days of the West were over and that cowboys and Indians had become historical figures. The first version of this statue was created in 1894 and was lost over time. He exhibited his larger-than-life sized plaster statue of The End of the Trail at the 1915 Panama-Pacific Exposition of 1915 held in San Francisco. Fraser hoped that someday the sculpture would be cast in bronze and permanently placed overlooking the Pacific Ocean.

Fraser's wife, Laura Gardin Fraser was also a talented artist. In 1926 she worked with her husband to design the Oregon Trail Commemorative Half-Dollar. This special coin has a Native American portrait on one side and a Conestoga wagon on the other side. James Earle Fraser died in 1953 at his home in Westport, Connecticut. He was 77 years old. Today his works of art continue to bend our hearts and minds to the Great Plains' original inhabitants.

Photographed
EDWARD S. CURTIS

Edward Sheriff Curtis traveled extensively throughout the Great Plains and Plateau regions of the United States taking thousands of photos. During this time he photographed some of the best-known Native Americans in history including the Sioux Sub-chief Red Hawk and the Nez Perce Chief Joseph.

In the summer of 1900 by invitation of George Bird Grinnell, Edward S. Curtis traveled to Montana to witness the annual sun dance of the Blood, Blackfeet and Algonquin tribes. He described the event as wild, terrifying, and elaborately mystifying. This experience profoundly affected Curtis and served as a major impetus for the development of the North American Indian project.

Curtis returned to the Great Plains and Plateau regions of the United States numerous times during his fieldwork for The North American Indian. It was at this time that he photographed some of the best known Native Americans in history, among them Red Hawk, a sub-chief of the Ogalala Sioux and the subject of one of Curtis' best known photographs, An Oasis in the Badlands.

Peyote Drummer (1927)
"The Peyote cult as it exists today can be considered in many ways as the most interesting religious organization among the North American Indians. The cult is predicated upon the use of peyote, a variety of cactus growing in Texas and northern Mexico. An important feature of the ceremony is the eating of the peyote "button", the small core at the center of the plant. No Indian custom has been the subject of greater controversy or has led to the adoption of more laws and regulations with a view of abolishing it, largely because its effects have been misunderstood by white people."

Huka'-Lowapi-Fire Carrier Bringing the Skull (1908)
This image shows the final preparations for the Huka-lowapi ceremony. According to Edward Curtis, "the principal purpose of Huka-lowapi is to implant in the initiate the virtues of kindness, generosity, hospitality, truthfulness, fairness, honesty. At the same time it is a prayer for continued prosperity – for abundance of food, for health, strength, and moral well-being as a people."

History

Red Whip-Atsina (1908)

"Born in 1858 near Fort McGinnis, Montana. At the age of seventeen he went out on his first war expedition, going against the Sioux. The enemy was camped at Lodgepole creek, and the Atsina attacked them at dawn, capturing several horses. Red Whip was in the lead of the charge and took a few of the animals single-handed… Red Whip was scouting on Tongue river with General Miles, when the Sioux charged a small body of soldiers, routing them. Red Whip says he stood firm and stopped the onrushing enemy until the troops escaped. His medicine, given to him by an uncle, is a strip of otter-fur."

During one visit in 1907 Curtis spent several days traversing the area surrounding the Little Bighorn River and the famous Custer Battlefield site. He was joined by three Crow Indians who had served as scouts for Custer right up to the battle on June 25, 1876, thirty-one years before. Through these meetings, as well as others with Red Hawk and a group of Cheyenne who fought along side the Sioux in the battle, Curtis was able to piece together a more complete account of Custer's Last Stand. In it he determined that Custer was partially responsible for the outcome of the massacre.

Curtis also had an opportunity to photograph perhaps the best known Native American of all time. Chief Joseph of the Nez Perce visited Seattle in 1903 to lecture on behalf of his people. He visited the Curtis Studio and sat for a portrait session. The resulting images are prominently featured in Volume and Portfolio VIII and were produced less than one year before Joseph's death.

In a Piegan Lodge (1910)

"Little Plume with his son Yellow Kidney occupies the position of honor, the space at the rear opposite the entrance. The picture is full of suggestion of the various Indian activities. In a prominent place lie the ever-present pipe and its accessories on the tobacco cutting-board. From the lodge-poles hang the buffalo-skin shield, the long medicine-bundle, an eagle-wing fan, and deerskin articles for accoutering the horse. The upper end of the rope is attached to the intersection of the lodge-poles, and in stormy weather the lower end is made fast to a stake near the centre of the floor space."

ANOTHER BOOK BY LINDA LITTLE WOLF

GREAT SPIRIT HORSE

Follow the Great Spirit Horse on his journey across the Great Plains. Enjoy his adventures and watch him receive magical gifts from the other creatures. His story has been told for many generations. This richly woven legendary tale is now in print to be enjoyed by everyone.

For more information, visit www.pelicanpub.com.

Great Spirit Horse is also available as a collectible model from Breyer Animal Creations.

Photo Credits

Page(s)	Provided by
11, 25, 42, 45-46, 57, 82, 86-90, 95-96	
	Wendy Wilson, Ocala, FL
10, 17, 28, 33-36, 38-41, 44, 47, 50, 52-53, 59, 61-67, 69, 76-78, 80-81, 83, 91, 98-99, 108-110, 120-121	
	Edward S. Curtis
104-107, 126-127	Robert Vavra
50, 52, 54-57, 61, 68, 100-101	
	Time Life Books, *The American Indians Series*
14, 85	Prairie Edge, Rapid City, SD
28	Buffalo Bill Musuem
58	Hudson's Bay Archive
67	Paul M. Rackza
108	Alberta Provincial Archives
112	Rich Paolello
119	US Government Archives
119	National Institute of the Arts
8, 12-13, 30, 43, 59, 68, 73, 79, 81, 83, 114-117	
	unknown

Illustration Credits

Page	Provided by
cover	David Behrens
9, 18-21, 23, 26-27, 31, 51, 94, 96-97	
	Kimberly Spatrisano
70	Howard Terpning
92	Walter McClintock
93	George Catlin
102	Alfred Jacob Miller
16, 24, 28, 32, 37, 71, 74-75, 84, 89	
	unknown

STATES

Mitakueye Oyasin

(We all all related)

We all share this earth as family;
you, me, and our equine brothers
and sisters. Go with peace.

— Linda Little Wolf